Gospel of Fulfilment

Exploring the Gospel of Matthew

— PATRICK WHITWORTH —

Sacristy
Press

Sacristy Press
PO Box 612, Durham, DH1 9HT

www.sacristy.co.uk

First published in 2019 by Sacristy Press, Durham

Sacristy Limited, registered in England & Wales, number 7565667

British Library Cataloguing-in-Publication Data
A catalogue record for the book is available from the British Library

ISBN 978-1-78959-044-9

Foreword

Patrick Whitworth is a man of profound faith and humility. As priest he is, in one sense, a "behind-the-scenes" pastor—deeply prayerful, with a firm yet often hidden hand on the tiller, always enabling others to grow in their faith. His personal and public life are grounded in his love for the word of God. His intellectual rigour and knowledge underpin his quiet authority. He exudes a confidence in Jesus, his Lord, and so enables others to know that presence. It is this same intellectual rigour that shines in his writing, so contributing more insight and wisdom, to help us all grow in our faith. This in turn helps us to earth that faith authentically in everyday life.

This is the second of his books on the Gospels. His first, *Gospel for the Outsider*, shows how Luke—a Gentile—brings in other outsiders.[1] This present book, as Patrick says in his Introduction, sets out another perspective on our redemption. "Matthew comprehensively demonstrates that Jesus fulfils everything that is written about the Messiah in the Old Testament, if only the Jews have eyes to see." Patrick does two things in this book: he identifies those people Matthew aims to reach, and he places Matthew in the "grand picture"—the complete gospel. There is only one, worldwide, saving network in Jesus Christ's name. As all who teach know, no one can please all people. It is the four Gospels *together* that give the complete picture.

Fulfilment is an important part of the truth of Jesus. If we think of the timeline from creation (the Bible is clear that there is a Creator, whenever and however this happened) to the end of the world (whenever that will be), then on that timeline there is One Man, One Moment—Jesus.

The time window between creation and Jesus, the Old Testament era, is characterized by:

- God's presence on earth being defined within the custodianship of one chosen race—the Israelites;
- humankind being shown to be unable to "make the mark" on its own and to live to God's standard;
- the recording of multiple prophecies pointing towards Jesus.

In the era we are now in, the New Testament era:

- Jesus has opened the way back to the Father;
- it is now time, he says, to "go out and tell this gospel to all nations";
- Jesus says, "Now I am with you always. I will send you the Holy Spirit." We see him at work when we look.

God wants us to return, to harness our wills to him, to adore, obey, praise, pray. We can, in Jesus' name. That has been the Creator's desire ever since the beginning. Matthew is placed at the start of the New Testament, although Mark was written first, because Matthew's Gospel bridges the two eras, presenting Jesus as the fulfilment of the Old Testament prophecies. And with this comes hope, healing and eternal life.

Matthew is Jewish, writing to a Jewish readership. Patrick, with deft scriptural criticism, helps us to imagine Matthew's intention. We see his editorial action. We are encouraged to see the mind and faith of the Gospel writer:

- to talk in the language of a new church community;
- to give these disciples a training manual for living;
- to show to the Jewish readership that this man Jesus, and this Gospel, are now for all nations.

Matthew sets out to enable the transition from old to new. Patrick helps us to see God as real and dynamic, closely involved, through Jesus, in the human lives of the world. He provides many references, including cross-referring to the other three Gospels. So while this book sets out to describe Matthew's viewpoint—why he lays out his Gospel in the way that he does—the book also contributes to the one gospel of One Man, our

Saviour, the complete picture being provided by four different accounts. A study guide helps to enable this.

Here is another contribution to the contemporary writing about Jesus as our Saviour. It is important in our present era, when there is such a need to reawaken faith. We are living in a society that is increasingly questioning, and at the same time increasingly seeking after truth and meaning. I believe that today's young people are reading Scripture in a clear-minded way, apparently without the sceptical "baggage" of their parents' generation. Determined atheism just does not ring true. Science will not explain everything! This book helps set out the evidence base for our Lord—the certainty of hope in the mystery of God—and looks ahead to a time when, in reply to someone saying to us, "Oh, this religion is not for me," or "I'm not a church goer," we will be able to say, "Oh really, why not? There is so much evidence . . . "

The Revd Canon Nigel Rawlinson
University Chaplain, University of Bath
February 2019

Preface

This is the second of a series of guided studies on the Gospels, which can be used either for personal study or in a Bible study group. The first, *Gospel for the Outsider: The Gospel in Luke & Acts*, was published in 2014 and has proved popular.

The purpose of this series is to show the particular standpoint of the different Gospel writers. They all wanted to communicate the extraordinary and life-changing story of Jesus of Nazareth, and his claim on all our lives as the unique Son of God, the Saviour and the Lord. Beyond that, each Gospel had an individual purpose. Each evangelist (Gospel writer) had a different experience and wrote with a particular group in mind. And of the four, Matthew—in some ways—is the least easy to grasp. His is the longest, and the most Jewish, of the four Gospels.

Mark's Gospel was the first to be written, perhaps around AD 65. It may have been written in Rome. In a succinct way—it is almost half the length of Matthew—it shows Jesus as the Lord. In a world dominated by the thought and expectation that Caesar was the Lord, here was a bold and revolutionary idea. Indeed, here was a new expression of power. Mark's Gospel is told with verve and skill. Both Luke and Matthew plunder its content and narrative for their own.

Luke and Matthew wrote their Gospels next: Luke with the experience of being a Gentile, a companion of the apostle Paul, and a doctor—well used to human need. As I wrote in my commentary on Luke's Gospel, he has a consistent eye for the way Jesus makes an impact on the outsider: the lost, the ostracized, the sinner, the Samaritan, the pagan centurions, and even the dying thief. Matthew, it seems, is writing primarily for a Jewish readership: convincing them that Jesus of Nazareth was and is the Messiah, the one who has fulfilled the prophecies of the Old Testament. His is therefore the *Gospel of Fulfilment*, and as such was placed first in the New Testament by the Church Fathers, saying thereby, "Everything promised in the Old Testament is fulfilled in Jesus: the law, the sacrificial system, the wisdom-teaching". Jesus holds all these threads, and this is exhibited in Matthew's Gospel. Indeed, the Sermon on the Mount both fulfils the law and surpasses the wisdom of the Old Testament. Furthermore, Matthew wrote his Gospel as a discipleship manual for all followers of Jesus, and as a leadership manual for all leaders of Christian communities.

I hope in the next few years to complete this series, writing on Mark and culminating with John. How might these two studies be titled? We shall see.

In producing this study guide, I would once again like to thank Benedict Books for preparing the book for publication, Sacristy Press for continuing with the project, Nigel Rawlinson (a friend and colleague) for generously writing the Foreword, and my wife Olivia for her interest in my writing, but more importantly in the writings of the evangelists.

Patrick Whitworth

14 February 2019
The feast of St Cyril and St Methodius, Missionaries to the Slavs

Contents

Introduction

Most Christians have a favourite Gospel. Many are drawn to the immediacy and brevity of Mark. Others love the profound simplicity and hidden depths of John: the layered conversations and the revelatory teaching, as in the Upper Room. Still others are drawn to the humanity of Luke's portrayal of Jesus, with his evident concern for the weak, the humble, the outsider and the outcast. Perhaps fewer are drawn to Matthew, with its forbidding opening genealogy, its evident Jewishness and its challenging length. Yet only Matthew has the Sermon on the Mount, and he includes many unique parables, such as the Sheep and the Goats. Without Matthew we would miss many of the jewels of Jesus' teaching. The four Gospels *together* provide an all-round description of Jesus and his ministry, but each Gospel writer provides something unique and distinctive in the telling of his story.

What follows in this short book is not a comprehensive description and commentary on the Gospel of Matthew, but a view of the Gospel from its "unique selling point", that is, *what distinguishes it* more than anything else from Mark, Luke and John, and what it seeks especially to communicate, both to the contemporaries of the writer and to us today, living as we do in a very different milieu from that of first-century, probably Jewish Christians.[2] In this series of study books on the Gospels, Luke's is described as the *Gospel for the Outsider*, while Matthew's is seen as the *Gospel of Fulfilment*. That is to say, Matthew comprehensively demonstrates that Jesus fulfils everything written about the Messiah in the Old Testament, if only the Jews have eyes to see. This, I believe, is the key to understanding Matthew's Gospel, and the theme we shall seek to elaborate by looking at most, if not all, of the Gospel's material.

First we need to find some kind of overview of the Gospel itself by standing back and looking at the entire mountain range of its narratives and teachings, before trying to scale some of the individual peaks.

Nevertheless, the overall theme behind all this mountaineering is *fulfilment*.

One of the strongest features of the Gospel of Matthew is its Jewishness. This could be said of at least three of the Gospel writers. Mark is a Jew, probably living in Rome and writing for a Gentile and Jewish audience in the Empire, and especially in the capital. John is a Jew almost certainly writing in Ephesus for Hellenistic Jews tempted by Gnosticism, hence the theme of the opening prologue. Matthew, whose identity we discuss later, is probably a Christian Jew writing in Antioch, in the Province of Syria. Luke could well be a Gentile, also writing in Antioch, having accompanied Paul on his missionary journeys, and writing his two-volume work for Theophilus (Luke 1:3 and Acts 1:1), a Roman enquirer or convert.

Matthew is a Jewish writer aiming at a predominantly Jewish audience, who form the majority of the church where they worship. He writes about issues that are of special interest and concern to Jewish followers of Jesus. He, like Paul in his preaching to Jewish synagogues (at the synagogue in Pisidian Antioch, for example; Acts 13:32–33), says that Jesus is the fulfilment of all God's promises. On every occasion Matthew shows how the Old Testament is linked to the life and ministry of Jesus. He demonstrates vividly Jesus' attitude to the Torah, the Old Testament law, and the traditions of the scribes and Pharisees. He describes dramatically, with no holds barred, the attitude of Jesus to the Jewish authorities, in his excoriating teaching in Chapter 23 about the spirituality of the Pharisees. Matthew's principal argument, as with the Epistle to the Hebrews (also written for Jewish Christians), is that Jesus is the fulfilment of all that has gone before: the promises to the Patriarchs, the calling of a nation special to God, the Exodus, the Law, the Temple, and the Prophets, who themselves looked forward to his coming. In fulfilling all these aspects of Judaism, Jesus opens the kingdom of heaven to the Gentiles. All that has gone before finds its fulfilment in Jesus.

Issues uppermost in Jewish minds at the time Matthew was writing were as follows: How does Jesus' teaching relate to the Law? What is the right use of the Sabbath? What is the future of the Temple? How can Jew and Gentile be included in a single community? Is Jesus really the expected Messiah? These were questions for Jews both inside and outside the church in the second half of the first century, and they are answered in this Gospel.

Among the indications of Matthew's Jewishness, or his Semitic bias, are his use of Semitic words like "*raka*" ("fool"), which remains untranslated in Matthew 5:22, or "*korbanas*" in 27:6, meaning "treasury". Matthew assumes familiarity with these Jewish terms. R. T. France writes:

> In its constant reference to the Old Testament, its strong Jewish flavouring, its explicit discussions of the conflict between Jesus and the Jewish authorities, it forms a fitting 'bridge' between Old and New Testaments, a constant reminder to Christians of 'the rock from which they were hewn'.[3]

Although Mark's was the first Gospel to be written, the church put Matthew first in its New Testament canon because it forms a bridge between the Old and New Testaments.

Not only is there a clear emphasis on the fulfilment of all that is promised in the Old Testament in the person of Jesus the Messiah, but there are several other strong characteristics to the Gospel as well. These are the "ecclesial" nature of the Gospel, the sense of it being a training manual for disciples, and its imperative to take the message from the Jews to all nations. Firstly, Matthew's is the only Gospel to have the notion of "church" or "*ekklesia*" in it. From this we get the word "ecclesiastical", which tends to have associations—in English minds at least—with the fusty accretions of the institutional Church. "*Ekklesia*" literally means those who are called out by God in Christ, in other words, the church community. From soon after Pentecost, whether in Jerusalem or Antioch, or in the cities to which Paul travels on his missionary journeys, churches spring up possessing great diversity: in terms of slave and free, rich and poor, men and women, Jews and Gentiles. In fact, they really are new communities, quite different from all previous religious communities. Jewish worship, whether in the temple or the synagogue, tended to exclude the Gentiles, although in the temple area there was an outer court for the Gentiles and the synagogues did have their Gentile supporters, such as the centurion whose faith Jesus praised and who had built a synagogue for the Jews (see Luke 7:4–6 and Matthew 8:5ff.). Yet in the

church, all these barriers of ethnicity, race, religious heritage, sex and
social rank are to be dissolved into a single fellowship of disciples (see
Galatians 3:28–29). It is this new community Matthew is addressing in
his Gospel.

On two occasions Matthew specifically uses the word *"ekklesia"*
(16:18 and 18:17), once in reference to the church being built on Peter's
confession of Jesus as Messiah, and once in relation to church discipline.
In Matthew's Gospel there is much that is important for both church
leaders and members: teaching about the Sabbath and how to observe it
now they are Christians (12:1–14), and teaching about divorce (5:31–32;
19:3–9), which comes with the proviso that adultery may legitimately
terminate marriage. From the woman's point of view that must have been
revolutionary, although for economic reasons it is hard to envisage. Then
there is teaching about how to face persecution (Chapter 10), and about
distinguishing between true and false prophets, teachers and Messiahs
(7:15–20; 24:4–5,11,23–26). All this teaching is deliberately grouped
together to show how the church is to conduct itself in these areas.
Matthew's Gospel is a manual for church leadership and membership,
as well as being a Gospel demonstrating that Jesus is the Messiah foretold
in the Old Testament.

If Matthew's Gospel has a strong teaching and training element useful
for church life, it also has real missionary thrust and momentum. This
is made quite clear by the final chapter of the Gospel (28:16–20), which
unambiguously states—through Jesus' "Great Commission"—that this
news of the kingdom, the teaching that Jesus has given, is for all nations,
indeed for the whole world. However, the whole progression or trajectory
of the Gospel is not simply the positive idea that what began with the Jews
is now to be taken to the world, but is also that, because of their rejection
of Jesus as the Messiah, the Jewish authorities are to be judged. We cannot
escape the conclusion, in reading the Gospel, that Matthew, who is very
familiar with the narrative of the Old Testament, has come to the opinion
that the leaders of his nation have missed their opportunity, and that their
leadership has now been replaced by Christ himself. R. T. France wrote:

> What we see in Matthew is [rather] the uncomfortable tension
> in the mind of one who, brought up to value and love all that

> Israel has stood for, has come to the painful conclusion that the
> majority of his people have failed to respond to God's call to
> them, and that it is in a 'remnant', the minority group who have
> followed Israel's true Messiah, that God's purpose is now centred.[4]

The result of this rejection is that the gospel, as originally intended, is to go worldwide (see also Romans 11:11–12).

The person who is to be made known to all nations is the Jesus of the Gospel, who is described in four different ways. Firstly, he is the *Messiah*, the anointed one or Christ. The confession by Peter that Jesus is the Christ is the turning point of the Gospel, as it is in Mark also (Matthew 16:16; Mark 8:29). This confession lies at the heart of the Gospel, ending the earlier Galilean ministry, apart from some private teaching given to the disciples (Matthew 16:21–18:35), and preparing for the ministry in Judea and in Jerusalem. The recognition that Jesus is the Messiah, and therefore also the *Son of David*, through this confession by the leading apostle, is the turning point of this narrative, just as it is the turning point of Paul's life on the road to Damascus. There is, then, a continuing need to prove that Jesus is the Messiah from the Scriptures, as indeed Paul does in his preaching of Christ to the Jews (Acts 9:22).

The second main title by which Jesus is known in the Gospel is *Son of Man*, clearly Jesus' favourite way of describing himself. It is a title or description found in Ezekiel and Daniel in the Old Testament (see Ezekiel 2:1,3; 3:1 and Daniel 7:13). The title has clear prophetic and eschatological connotations, meaning that it is connected to the prophetic call of Ezekiel. In Daniel, the vision of the Son of Man is of a human figure given full authority to enact God's will (compare Matthew 10:23; 16:27–28; 19:28; 24:27,30; 25:31; 26:64; 28:18). Yet Jesus attaches new significance to the title, not only by speaking of the glory to come (as in Daniel), but also of his future sufferings and humiliation.

The third main title for Jesus used by Matthew is *King*. It is this title ("King of the Jews") which appears on the charge fixed to the cross on which Jesus is crucified (27:11,29,37,42). For Matthew, Jesus is the true king, for whom the wise men search and whom they then worship at his nativity (2:2,11). Once again, Jesus fulfils all the ideals of kingship found in the Old Testament. Jesus announces the coming of the kingdom (9:35).

He demonstrates it by his works of power. He exemplifies its leadership by humble service. The mission of Jesus is to establish God's kingdom: God in control. Much of the Gospel tells us what this kingdom is like, and does so through the use of parables (see Matthew 13). His disciples are to seek his kingdom above all else (6:33). They are to pray for the coming of his kingdom (6:9–13). Finally, to underline the Jewishness of the Gospel, Matthew prefers (in the main) the title "kingdom of heaven" rather than "kingdom of God". For the Jew, the name of God is rarely spoken. However, there are some instances of the kingdom of God (rather than heaven) being mentioned (see 12:28; 19:24; 21:31,43; 26:29 which refer to "my Father's kingdom"). What is clear from this is that Matthew envisages Jesus as a king who is inaugurating a new kingdom, a fulfilment of all that is promised from David onwards.

Matthew's final title for Jesus is the *Son of God*. This takes us beyond a purely human designation for Christ to one that signifies divinity. It is not a title Jesus uses about himself, but it is alluded to at the time of the nativity (2:15). It is used by the Father (3:17; 17:5), by demons with their supernatural knowledge (8:29), by Satan (4:3,6), and by Jesus' opponents, especially around the time of his crucifixion (26:63; 27:40,43,54). Finally, it is a title ascribed to Jesus in the Great Commission in Matthew 28:19.

The Gospel is therefore written to make Jesus known as the Messiah, the Son of Man, the King, and finally the Son of God, in the context of fulfilling all that has been promised to Israel beforehand, and as an instruction manual for a church in the process of formation. It is a Gospel demonstrating that everything promised to Israel by YAHWEH is fulfilled in Jesus. If this is the driving purpose behind the Gospel and its unique selling point, we must turn to the question of how it was assembled, by whom, when, and what sources were available to Matthew.

Scholars generally agree that Mark's was the first Gospel to be written.[5] It is probable that Matthew had a manuscript copy of Mark's Gospel either to hand or readily available to him. This being the case, Matthew uses Mark's Gospel as a chief source in the writing of his Gospel for his own community, and with the purpose that we have already tried to explain. The community is a church, quite possibly in Syria or Antioch, and the Gospel is written for this church's leaders and members, and indeed for all churches like it. The Gospel seeks primarily to demonstrate the way

Jesus fulfils the Jewish law and prophets, in a way in which the Jewish community leaders, the scribes and Pharisees, do not.

Matthew, however, does not simply edit Mark's Gospel with his own objectives in mind and without the help of other material. He has other sources on which to draw. Scholars have shown that ninety per cent of Mark's Gospel is found in Matthew, whereas only seventy-nine per cent is found in Luke. Both Gospels share a further twenty-four per cent of common material, meaning that they share either another written source called "Q" (from the German "*Quelle*", meaning "source"), or they share a common oral tradition.[6] What is clear is that in both Matthew and Luke, the use of Q material is encased within the structure supplied by Mark.[7] Scholars debate how much of a written source Q was, arguing that it might have been an oral one. In relation to his use of Mark, Matthew constructs a smoother and less abrupt narrative by editing out Mark's frequent use of words like "immediately" or "again". Other editorial shifts in the hands of Matthew are his lengthier explanation of why Jesus is baptized (3:14–15); the committing of adultery as being legitimate grounds for divorce (5:32); his addition of the Old Testament prophecy "I desire mercy, not sacrifice" (Hosea 6:6), to stories gleaned from Mark (9:13; 12:7); his promotion of Peter as the leading apostle and the Rock on whom the church will be built (Matthew 16:17–19); and his addition of a fierce condemnation of the Jewish leaders to Mark's Parable of the Tenant Farmers (Matthew 21:43–45). If Matthew was able to draw on alternative traditions of the Jesus story (alongside his possession of Mark's Gospel), we would have to say these additions are theologically motivated to underscore the purpose and perspective of his Gospel.

So the sources for Matthew are Mark's Gospel and the material (either oral or written) called Q; finally, about thirty per cent of the Gospel is unique to Matthew. This last section of material is, in part, what makes Matthew distinctive, in the same way as the thirty per cent peculiar to Luke makes *his* Gospel distinct (for example, his infancy narratives, parables such as the Prodigal Son, Dives and Lazarus, and the Good Samaritan, as well as different narratives around the Passion, such as the response of the thieves crucified with Jesus and the remarkable narrative of the Road to Emmaus). The notable parts of Matthew's Gospel unique to him are *his* infancy narratives, parts of the Sermon on the

Mount, parables such as the Sheep and the Goats (25:31–46), and Jesus' excoriating indictment of the spirituality of the Pharisees and teachers of the law in Chapter 23. This is distinctive material, threaded by Matthew into his editorial purpose of showing Jesus as the fulfilment of the Old Testament, of giving instruction to a recently birthed and heavily Jewish church, and of affirming that the message is one for the whole world.

Before looking at the shape and structure of the Gospel, we move to its authorship and date. This Gospel, like the others, is anonymous. The traditional view of its authorship is that it was written by Matthew, the former tax collector also known as Levi. Jesus calls Matthew from his tax collector's booth to be a disciple and apostle (Matthew 9:9–13;10:2–4). That story is recorded by Matthew, and in a slightly different form in Luke 5:27–28. Little else is said about Matthew, who appears as a sociable, well-connected figure who generously entertains Jesus and his friends, fellow tax collectors and "sinners" at a feast (Matthew 9:10; Mark 2:15; Luke 5:29—"a great banquet"). He is probably a Greek speaker who works for the Roman administration. He is known as Levi in Mark and Luke (Mark 2:13–17; Luke 5:27–32), indicating that he probably comes from the tribe of Levi, which has the responsibility for maintaining the tabernacle and subsequently the temple (see Deuteronomy 18:1–8). This much we know about Matthew from the Gospels.

The tradition of his authorship of this eponymous Gospel comes from the Early Church Fathers. The principal source here is the extensive use made of Matthew (and attributed to him) by the Apostolic Fathers, writing in the early second century. Indeed, Matthew's is the most frequently quoted Gospel in the writings of the Apostolic Fathers, especially Ignatius, Bishop of Antioch (d. 108), who was martyred in Rome. It is in a statement by Papias, Bishop of Hierapolis, near Laodicea, that the most definite yet problematic attribution to Matthew is made. In Book III of the *History of the Church*, covering the first three centuries, Eusebius records Papias as saying, "Matthew compiled the oracles in the Hebrew dialect, and everyone translated them as best he could."[8] This statement is hardly a ringing endorsement by Papias. For one thing, he was—by modern standards—a notoriously inaccurate historian. R. T. France says that this ascription of the Gospel is "full of ambiguities".[9] The quotation from Papias gives the impression that Matthew assembled a number of sayings of Jesus (the Greek word used in the original text of Eusebius is "*logia*"), put together in a loose composition of Hebrew sayings or stories, and that the further assembling of a coherent Gospel fell to Matthew's followers, who also translated it into Greek, the *lingua franca* of the Empire. We simply cannot be sure. That the earliest patristic comment on Matthew is so loose in its definition leaves us with the possibility that Matthew assembled the material, reflecting both his own strong Jewish background and his desire to show that Jesus completely fulfils all the Old Testament hopes of the Messiah, and that it was then left to others who knew him and worked with him to put these sayings into a final form. What does seem to be well attested and received by the Early Church is that the Gospel, however it was finally formed, was the result of Matthew's collection and convictions, and that this apostolic witness was widely accepted in the church—by Papias, Ignatius, and Origen.[10] In conclusion, the outcome that best suits the evidence is that Matthew was probably the main compiler of the Gospel, but its production from a collection of sayings and stories—collected alongside Mark's Gospel and Q—may have been the work of Matthew and a group around him, as part of a strongly Jewish church, possibly in the region of Antioch around the year AD 80.

The dating of the Gospel cannot be precise. The Gospel writers all have apostolic connections, or are themselves apostles, so the Gospels must come from within the lifespan of someone who knew Jesus directly (or indirectly, as in the case of Luke). Most modern scholars believe Matthew was written in the final twenty years of the first century. A few clues are provided from internal and external evidence in the Gospel. Since Matthew's Gospel includes most of Mark's Gospel, written between AD 64 and 70 in Rome, where Mark was living with the apostle Peter from whom he gleaned his material for the Gospel, Matthew's Gospel must have been written after the year 70. For Matthew to be either the author or originator of the Gospel means that by AD 80 he would be in his late seventies. His age can be guessed from the fact that he would not be a tax collector before his early twenties, given the responsibility of the job as well as the social pressure it carried (working as a Jew for an occupying regime and as a Levite in an unclean and "sinful" profession). If this is the case, then Jesus called him in his twenties around the year AD 28. Furthermore, the destruction of Jerusalem—following the Jewish

Rebellion of 65–70—by the armies of Vespasian and Titus, is thought by scholars to affect the language in Matthew 22:7, a verse from the Parable of the Wedding Banquet, in which the king reacts to the non-attendance of his guests: "The king was enraged. He sent his army and destroyed those murderers and burned their city."

Taken together, the evidence seems to place the composition of the Gospel in a period from AD 75 at the earliest to around AD 80 at the latest. Nothing more definite can be stated. By this time the separation between Jew and Christian had grown more permanent. From the year 85 onwards Christians were effectively excluded from the synagogue by the insertion of a curse in the synagogue liturgy (the so-called "*Birkat ha-Minim*").[11] This would give further reason to assure anxious Christian Jews, put out of the synagogue, that Jesus is truly the Messiah, the fulfilment of all Old Testament Jewish expectation. In this context, Matthew's Gospel is a piece of apologetic literature defending the Messiahship of Jesus at a time of increasing distance and animosity between Jew and Christian, at the level of ordinary synagogue worship. It is important to remember this while reading it.

Finally, we must sketch in the structure of Matthew's Gospel. Many structural patterns have been proposed; there seems to be one simple overarching structure, however, within which other rhythms of presentation are discernible and favoured by the author. The overall structure is Markan: that is, the narrative is based on the pattern provided by Mark in his Gospel. This comprises:

- *Introduction* (Matthew 1:1–4:11; Mark 1:1–13);
- *Ministry in Galilee* (Matthew 4:12–13:58; Mark 1:14–6:13);
- *Wider ministry in the north* (Matthew 14:1–16:12; Mark 6:14–8:26);
- *Towards Jerusalem* (Matthew 16:13–20:34; Mark 8:27–10:52);
- *Confrontation in Jerusalem* (Matthew 21:1–25:46; Mark 11:1–13:37);
- *Passion and resurrection* (Matthew 26:1–28:20; Mark 14:1–16:8).

This structure captures not only the geographical movement of Jesus' ministry from Galilee to Jerusalem, but also contrasts the enthusiasm of the crowds in Galilee, where the kingdom is made known in word and action, with the hostility of the authorities in Jerusalem, where Jesus' Passion and resurrection take place. While this is the overarching structure of the Gospel and thus similar to Mark (and Luke), there are literary devices which form sub-sections within it. One such device is Matthew's use of the phrase, "From that time on Jesus began . . ." (see 4:17 and 16:21). Both these occurrences begin new phases of Jesus' ministry: the first after his initial introduction to Israel through his birth, baptism, and temptations, and the second following the confession of Jesus as the Messiah by the leading apostle, Peter, and the announcement of his forthcoming betrayal and death. On this basis, one scholar gives the Gospel three main sections:

- *The person of Jesus Christ* (Matthew 1:1–4:16);
- *The ministry and proclamation of Jesus the Messiah* (Matthew 4:17–16:20);
- *The suffering, death, and resurrection of Jesus the Messiah* (Matthew 16:21–28:20).

In many ways this scheme (provided by J. D. Kingsbury) simply underscores and defines the Markan structure of the Gospel.[12]

Another scheme, not too dissimilar, is also based around a recurring phrase in the Gospel: "When Jesus had finished saying these things . . ." This is used to punctuate the end of major sections of Jesus' teaching in the Gospel: about discipleship (Matthew 7:28); about mission (11:1); about the kingdom of heaven (13:53); about relationships (19:1); and about the future (26:1). It is, therefore, a further device used to separate Jesus' teaching into discernible sections before the narrative or itinerary moves the reader on again.

Other scholars, like B. W. Bacon, have wanted to press the point that in the Gospel there are five sections of teaching broken up by five narratives or itineraries of Jesus, and that these correspond to the five books of the law, replacing them with new teaching about the identity and calling of the people of God.[13] However attractive the theory might be theologically, it nevertheless artificially shapes the material in ways that are not always obvious.

What we are left with is a narrative that reflects the Markan shape. It is a story that moves from Galilee to Jerusalem, from enthusiastic response to redemptive rejection. It includes discernible sections of teaching, broken by stages on the way to the cross, on what it means to be part of the new community Jesus is creating, and it shows the fulfilment of the law, the temple, the sacrificial system, and the period of waiting for the Messiah. He has come and is now to be followed. It is time to see how this may be done.

CHAPTER 1

Discovering the True Identity of Jesus

Matthew 1:1–4:11

In recent years there has been an upsurge of interest in genealogy and tracing one's ancestry. This has been driven in part by the internet, with its powerful means of searching family histories, but also by the science of genetic recognition. When King Richard III's remains were traced by a university lecturer to a car park in Leicester, the former site of the Abbey where the king's mortally wounded body was taken after the Battle of Bosworth Field in 1485, the remains were identified through DNA sampling. A descendant of Richard III was found and DNA samples were taken, both from the skeleton under the car park and from the descendant. The samples were a perfect match, and the body was thus identified, more than five hundred years after his death, as that of Richard III. The DNA match, the location of the body in an abbey close to the battlefield, some malformation of the spine corroborated by contemporary records about Richard's physique, and a wound consonant with warfare all positively identified the skeleton as being that of the king.

Past ancestral records available digitally online, genetic testing and simple visual recognition: all are means of discovering our identity. Even the present Archbishop of Canterbury found that his father was not the person he thought he had been. Following a journalist's probe, and with his own co-operation in taking a genetic test, Justin Welby discovered that his father was in fact Sir Anthony Montague Browne, who had been a Private Secretary to Winston Churchill from 1952, and not Gavin Welby, who therefore became his stepfather. Identity—who we are, where our ancestors came from, and what they did with their lives—are of great interest to many people. This accounts for the growing interest in television programmes such as *Who Do You Think You Are?* in which people are gently exposed to the truth about their ancestry, often with very revealing and moving consequences.

It is not surprising, therefore, that Matthew, our Gospel writer, should identify his main subject, Jesus, at the outset. He does this in various ways: by placing Jesus in a genealogical tree; by giving us five scriptures which Jesus' nativity and early life fulfil; by recalling the account given to Joseph of the non-biological nature of Jesus' conception and birth; by highlighting the recognition of Jesus by wise astronomers (or perhaps even astrologers); by reflecting on the Old Testament resonance (or typology) of the Holy Family going down to Egypt as refugees; and finally by pointing to the identification of Jesus by John the Baptist. Matthew gives these six proofs, mostly in keeping with the distinctive Jewish tradition of identifying the coming of the Messiah. We shall explore each of these proofs in turn.

Genealogy

A genealogy can seem rather forbidding at the beginning of a book. It is not what we are accustomed to, but Matthew has good reason to begin his Gospel as he does (1:1–17). There are immediate echoes of the beginning of Genesis, where the author simply states, "In the beginning God created the heavens and the earth" (Genesis 1:1; see also Chapter 5, a record of the original human ancestry following Adam). Matthew's writing here resonates with Genesis through his literal use of the Greek word "*genesis*" (Matthew 1:1), translated in English editions as "genealogy", but with other possible meanings such as "origin" or even "new creation".[14] If we take the idea of "new creation" rather than "genealogy", something much larger is being proposed. What Matthew is saying is that with the advent of Jesus, who is descended from Abraham and David, a whole new creation is beginning, and it is one that complements the original creation recorded in Genesis.

Matthew is introducing a record (or "*biblos*" in the Greek) of this new creation. He is introducing us to none less than the harbinger or bringer of this new creation, after the original creation has failed in Adam.

Indeed, Christ will regenerate humanity after the failure of Adam. That is a far more arresting idea than the rather plain statement, "Here is Jesus' family tree." Nevertheless, Jesus' ancestry is important for identifying who he was and is. What we have here, then, is a confluence of two ideas about origin: firstly, the beginning of a new creation brought about by Jesus, and secondly, a record of the origin of Jesus himself. These ideas go together well because only Jesus can effect a new creation, because of who he is and his lineage, which Matthew shows as being both human and divine. This is the message of the Gospel.

Matthew now sets Jesus in the context of Jewish history, with the purpose of announcing that a new age is dawning. He gives a symbolic and historical genealogy, which is not fully comprehensive but is deeply theological. The structure Matthew uses is of three separate sets of fourteen generations, although the periods covered by these three sets are very unequal: Abraham to David (800 years); David to the Exile (450 years); and Jeconiah to Joseph (600 years). R. T. France concludes, "It seems then that Matthew's list, like some other biblical genealogies, is selective, and that the scheme of three fourteens is doing something other than recording statistical data."[15] The scheme of fourteen generations, which incidentally misses out four members of dynastic succession in the period from David to the Exile, is more theological than historical.[16]

In numerology—that is, significance through numbers—fourteen is twice seven. The perfect Jewish number is seven, with the original temple menorah having seven branches (Exodus 25:31–37), although later, in the Second Temple, this candelabrum increased to nine branches. There are also seven days of creation. Three groups of fourteen make six sevens; so the seventh seven would denote the perfect age, beginning with the coming of the Messiah. Equally, in Jewish interpretation or "*gematria*", values are given to letters. David's name consists of three consonants, DWD, of which the numerical value is four (D), six (W) and four (D). The result is fourteen.

What does all this mean in terms of Matthew's theology? It probably means that what has preceded Jesus is now complete: the age of the patriarchs and the Exodus (from Abraham) is complete; the age of the monarchy (from David) is complete; and finally, the age of preparation and waiting for the Messiah (from the Exile until the present) is complete.

In other words, when the time has fully arrived for the coming of the Messiah (Galatians 4:4), he has come. These ages have been fulfilled, and the Messiah has come. A new age has dawned. A new creation has begun. The age of waiting is over.

Before we leave the genealogies, one further aspect of the record is worth marking, and that is the list of female ancestors of Jesus. Five are mentioned: Tamar, the daughter of Judah; Rahab, the prostitute; Ruth, the Moabite; Bathsheba, the wife of Uriah; and Mary, the wife of Joseph. They need not have been mentioned at all—it could have been a male-only ancestral tree, as is Luke's genealogy (Luke 3:23–38). Luke's is spread over sixty-five generations, taking Jesus' ancestors back to Adam. Yet Matthew chooses to include five women in his list. Why is that, and why these particular five (or four, if we exclude Mary)? The answer could be that each of these women is stigmatized through their relationship with their partners:

- Tamar's father-in-law is Judah, with whom she has sex;
- Rahab is a prostitute before marrying Salmon;
- Ruth (some say) seduces Boaz on the threshing floor;[17]
- Bathsheba is married to Uriah, but is seduced by David.

If this is the point, then Jesus' genealogy is one that points to grace rather than purity, to a divine plan rather than human deserving, the point being that God is prepared to forgive where there is—in the end—true trust in him. However, the point is more likely to be that in this Jewish family tree that gives rise to the Messiah, there are four women who are non-Israelites:

- Tamar is a Canaanite or Aramean;
- Rahab is a Canaanite;
- Ruth is a Moabite;
- Bathsheba is probably a Hittite.

The racial pedigree of these women (quite apart from the more culpable sexual history of many of their male partners), points to what Schweizer calls "the strange righteousness of God",[18] which is God's willingness to use sinful humans to bring about his righteous purpose, for indeed what else can he use? But more especially, what this genealogy proves is that the lineage of Jesus is not all Jewish, nor is it all pristine, and so this prepares Matthew's readers to believe that the Messiah and the Gospel are for all nations (Matthew 28:18–20), as indicated by the genealogy and the coming of the Magi to the nativity. Not only that, but it is a reminder to those who think themselves righteous that the Messiah comes into the world through the mess of human life. It is a point that Matthew will make over and over again.

This genealogy is symbolic, then, of all that is promised through Abraham and David, two of the greatest figures in Israelite history. Jesus will fulfil all that is promised to Abraham, in that he will be the descendant of Abraham who will bless all peoples on the earth (Genesis 12:3). He will also fulfil all that is promised to David, namely that God will establish through him an everlasting kingdom (Psalm 145:13) and that this kingdom will be inaugurated by Christ.

Jesus fulfils all that is promised to Abraham and David: he is their descendant both genealogically and theologically. But now Matthew goes one step further in identifying Jesus in his recounting of the birth narrative as told by Joseph, a descendant of the house of David and a true son of Abraham.

Virginal conception: the foundation of Christ's identity

The story of Joseph discovering that his betrothed, Mary, is pregnant, and the subsequent appearance of the angel to Joseph explaining that Mary is with child because of the Holy Spirit, is narrative theology of the greatest significance (1:18–25). It is a human story that carries the mystery of divine intervention and purpose to a point that defies rationality. While homely and domestic, it is also eternal and universal in its significance. Hence, in all the great works of art depicting the annunciation or the discovery by Joseph of what has happened to Mary, there is a sense of mystery and awe, evoking deep reflection and contemplation. The meaning of the event resonates with the heart as much as it instructs the mind.

While Luke concentrates on Mary's story, Matthew concentrates on Joseph's perspective. Whether Matthew chooses *not* to include Mary's account, in spite of knowing it, we simply cannot tell, but given the Jewish tenor of the Gospel, Joseph is the link between the promises made to David and their fulfilment in Jesus.

Joseph is well chosen as Mary's husband. He shows admirable qualities of righteousness, mercy, perception and strength. When he discovers that Mary is pregnant while betrothed to him and still living at her parents' house, he makes the natural assumption that, however uncharacteristic of Mary it might be, she has slept with another man and is expecting a child. He has two options open to him. He can either make a juridical –and hence public—case against her, causing her to bear her shame and the public opprobrium accompanying it, ruining her chances of any future marriage because she is an unfaithful single parent; or he can privately end the engagement for reasons that will become evident to all in her community. Because he is both a just ("*zaddik*") and merciful man,[19] he wants a separation or end to his engagement, but in a way that causes the least harm to Mary. One can only imagine the conversations between Mary and Joseph about her pregnancy, presumably with Mary trying to persuade him that her child is from a conception in which no man was involved, and more than that, that the Angel Gabriel told her that the child is the "Son of the Most High" and will be given the "throne of his father David" (Luke 1:32). Or perhaps she does not try to convince him at all but "pondering all these things in her heart" (Luke 2:19) keeps them to herself, trusting the outcome to God alone. In any event, an explanation to Joseph is forthcoming, but from another source.

While Joseph is ruminating or "inwardly considering"[20] all that has befallen him, including Mary's condition (and her extraordinary explanation for it), he too receives an angelic visitation. In Joseph's case, this is mediated through a dream in which an angel appears to him, addressing him as one descended from David (Matthew 1:20). He is given one stupendous fact and two commands.

The fact, upon which the identity of Jesus turns more than any other, is that the Holy Spirit was responsible for his conception. In a way that the Early Church Fathers strained to explain thereafter, the substance ("*ousia*") of the Godhead combines with the humanity of Mary to create within her womb a being who is completely God and completely man. In Christian doctrine this is normally referred to as the virgin birth, but now that we know far more about fertilization than the ancients it is, in fact, more accurately described as a virginal conception. One might assume that it is the seed of the Godhead and the egg of humanity combining to form a unique embryo, but we simply do not know the biological mechanics of this miracle of incarnation. Jesus is conceived by the Spirit and born of the Virgin Mary, as the Apostles' Creed puts it. The Greeks have a word for it—"*theotokos*"—making Mary the "bearer of God". Pope Leo writes thus in his *Tome* to Flavian, Patriarch of Constantinople, in 449:

> For the self-same who is very God is also very Man: and there is no illusion in this union, while the lowliness of man and the loftiness of Godhead meet together. For as "God" is not changed by the compassion exhibited, so "Man" is not consumed by the dignity bestowed. For each "form" does the acts which belong to it, in communion with the other; the Word, that is, performing what belongs to the Word, and the Flesh carrying out what belongs to the flesh.[21]

The origin of such a combination of divinity and humanity is conception by the Holy Spirit, and this is the astonishing fact that the angel announces to Joseph in his dream (1:20). Furthermore, Matthew affirms that this virginal conception leading to the birth of the Messiah, who is Immanuel, "God with us", should not totally surprise us, since it was prophesied by Isaiah (Matthew 1:22,23; Isaiah 7:14). This is further proof that the nativity of Jesus fulfils all that has been prophesied about him. The identity of Jesus as the only and unique One originates from his conception in Mary's womb by the Holy Spirit.

Because of this fact proclaimed to Joseph by the angel, he is now commanded to do two things: to take Mary home as his wife and to call his "son's" name Jesus, because "he will save his people from their sins" (1:21). Joseph does both. He takes Mary home, but has no sexual intercourse with her until she has given birth to Jesus (1:25), thus ensuring her virginity and setting her apart for the holy purpose to which she has been called. When the time comes, Joseph gives Jesus his name. "Jesus" is the Greek for the Hebrew "*Jeshua*", derived from the Hebrew verb "to save" ("*ys*") and the Hebrew noun "*yesua*", meaning "salvation". In Scripture, the meaning of a name denotes what that person is (see 1 Samuel 25:25). Jesus comes to save his people from their sins. He does not offer political liberation, but spiritual and moral freedom.

The identity of Jesus is carefully crafted in these opening chapters of Matthew's Gospel. The evidence of this unique enquiry of "Who do you think he is?" is exhaustively and conclusively assembled by Matthew. So far, we have been told that Jesus is both a son of Abraham and a son of David, fulfilling God's original promise to Abraham that God will bless all nations through him, and also God's promise to David that through his descendants an everlasting kingdom will be established. His unique divine/human being is established by the angelic news that he was conceived in Mary's body by the Holy Spirit. As a result, Joseph takes Mary home and waits to name the child Jesus.

In the next section of the nativity told by Matthew, Jesus is described as fulfilling Israel's calling to be a light to the nations and their struggle to bring this salvation to all people.

Journey of the Magi

The story of the arrival of the Magi in Bethlehem to offer their gifts to the infant Jesus, born king of the Jews, is multi-layered and textured. Whereas Luke has shepherds coming to the manger, representing a humbler profession despised by some Jews in the social milieu of the day (although redolent with biblical imagery associated with leadership: see Luke 2:8–20; Ezekiel 34; John 10:1–18), Matthew, in contrast, has the Magi—eastern mystics—coming to the manger throne to offer their gifts in worship (2:1–12).

The Magi carry a number of implications to the nativity account. They recall the Queen of Sheba bringing gold and spices to Solomon (1Kings 10:1–10). They represent the wisdom of the Gentiles, combining astronomy with some level of astrology in terms of identifying stars and reading significance into them. The Magi may be following a star or nova visible for seventy days in 5–4 BC and recorded by Chinese astrologers.[22] The Magi also echo the prophecy of Balaam, who recognized God's blessing on Israel and refused to curse it (Numbers 22:12; 24:15–17). Balaam likewise sees Israel as "a star" rising "out of Jacob" (Numbers 24:17b, Balaam's fourth prophecy or oracle over Israel). Like Balaam, the Magi are examples of individuals among the Gentiles with prophetic insight, albeit through the study of the stars. The Magi, like Balaam, are non-Israelites, holy men who come from beyond the Euphrates. And again, like Balaam, the Magi are pressured by a king. In their case it is Herod the Great. In Balaam's case it was Balak, king of Moab, the descendant of Esau, who sought to destroy God's chosen ones. If the coming of the shepherds in Luke's Gospel underscores Luke's central editorial conviction that the Gospel is for the outcast, the lost, the poor, and the despised, the coming of the Magi underscores Matthew's central editorial conviction that the Gospel is for all nations, for Jews and for Gentiles (see Matthew 28:19), especially since the Jews, as a nation, reject their Messiah. The Magi bring not only their worship to the manger-throne, but gifts prophetic of Christ's life. They indicate and announce his kingship (gold), his priesthood (frankincense), and his redemptive sufferings (myrrh). Like Balaam, they understand the nature and purpose of great David's greater Son, and declare it in their coming, their journey, their worship and their gifts.

It is also through the Magi that the motif of struggle and exodus is elevated. After all, it is their call on Herod for directions that activates his opposition and hatred of Jesus, who is described as a rival "King of the Jews". In the first instance, this visit to Herod is to ascertain where the new king heralded by the star is to be born. Although they follow the star believing it announces the birth of a new king of great significance, they presume to ask the local ruler for his knowledge of this event. Although this precipitates danger for the new-born king and the destruction of infants born in the vicinity over a two-year period, the visit to Herod has the purpose in the story of confirming the place of Jesus' birth. When Herod calls together the chief priests and teachers of the law, he asks them where the Messiah is to be born. The answer comes from Micah 5:2—the birth will be in Bethlehem. It is a quotation that Matthew slightly alters from the original, describing Bethlehem as being "in the land of Judah", not "Bethlehem Ephrathah" as in Micah's text. His purpose in this small alteration is probably to underscore that Jesus is of the line of Judah, born in this city of Judah. If the result of the Magi's call on Herod is, in part, to verify where this king is to be born, it is also the event whereby a struggle begins which comes to dominate the birth of Jesus.

From the outset, the birth of Jesus is welcomed both by those who are nearby, like the shepherds, and also by those who come from afar, like the Magi. Yet Jesus is also in grave danger from Herod. Now in the last year of his colourful, cruel and capricious rule, Herod brooks no rival, either to himself or to his family. So this infant king, whom the Magi have come to worship, must be killed at birth, in the same way Pharaoh commanded all male Israelite children in Egypt to be killed at their birth (Exodus 1:16). Here is another piece of biblical symmetry: in both Egypt and Judea a jealous and fearful king seeks to obliterate any rivals, whether a king, as in the case of Jesus, or a race, as in the case of the Israelites in Egypt. Herod feigns interest in Jesus' birth, but in fact he is implacably opposed to this new-born ruler. Thus when the Magi fail to return to tell Herod where to find the baby king, Herod determines to kill every infant in Bethlehem two years old or less, thereby slaughtering scores of children in the hope that one of them is his rival (2:13–18). The massacre of the innocents indicates the suffering that Jesus' life will bring, both to himself and to his followers.

In the narrative thus far, Matthew has shown that Jesus fulfils many Old Testament expectations. He is a son of Abraham and a son of David (1:1). He is conceived in Mary's womb through the power of the Holy Spirit in fulfilment of Isaiah's prophecy (1:20,23). Jesus fulfils the prophecy of Micah that the Messiah will be born in Bethlehem (Matthew 2:6; Micah 5:2). He also fulfils Hosea's prophecy that the Messiah will be called out of Egypt (Hosea 11:1), since the Holy Family flees there to avoid Herod's slaughter of innocent children born close to Jesus' own birthday. Matthew links the slaughter of the children in Bethlehem with a text from Jeremiah, lamenting the killing of innocent children at the time of Judah's exile (Matthew 2:18; Jeremiah 31:15). The words have no particular messianic content; they simply recall the death of innocent children and the excruciating grief at their loss as the Jews were marched from Ramah into exile in Babylon. Perhaps Ramah was the place of separation or the starting point where families were split apart before the journey to Babylon (Jeremiah 40:1). For Matthew, this lament is another sign of the fulfilment by Jesus of all that is predicted of his coming in the Old Testament.

Isaiah, Micah, Hosea and Jeremiah all testify to the events surrounding the birth and early years of the Messiah. They predict the circumstances of the nativity, giving scriptural validation to the origin and birth of the Messiah. Finally, Matthew searches for a text to corroborate the settling of Jesus in Nazareth (since, unlike Luke, Matthew does not appear to know that Mary and Joseph came from Nazareth and were returning to their home city, having gone to Bethlehem to be registered for tax purposes; Luke 2:1–5). Although Matthew claims the prophets say of the Messiah, "He will be called a Nazarene [a citizen of Nazareth]" (2:23),[23] there is in fact no mention of Nazareth in the Old Testament at all. Seeking to clarify this problem of exegesis, R. T. France says that "Perhaps [Matthew's] readers shared some more clearly agreed understanding of the meaning of the word *Nazoraios* and of what aspect of 'the prophets' Matthew was here appealing to, but if so it is not now available to us."[24]

In any event, as a result of the all-clear to return to Israel after the death of Herod being given to Joseph in a dream (2:19–20), the family travel back to Israel, not to Judah where Herod's son Archelaus reigns, but to Galilee instead. And it is from here, some twenty-five years later at the beginning of his public ministry, that Jesus is once again publicly identified, this time by his forerunner, John the Baptist, who acclaims him as the one who is greater than him (3:11). It is the final piece of identification Matthew gives us at the outset of the Gospel in this so-called *Book of Origin*, and we shall return to the witness of John the Baptist later.

So Jesus is clearly identified as the Messiah to his mainly Jewish readers (see 1:1,16,17,18; 2:4). The circumstances of his conception and birth are prophesied by the Jewish Scriptures. Matthew's focus is clear: the Messiah has come, his kingdom is coming, and he fulfils all that the Old Testament contains, not least the Torah or law. Now the Messiah must lay the foundations of his ministry and work on earth.

CHAPTER 2

Laying the Foundations

Matthew 3:13–4:25

After identifying and introducing the Messiah in the opening chapters of his Gospel, Matthew now shows Jesus laying the foundations of his ministry. This foundation-laying has four parts: Jesus' baptism, his temptations, his early preaching and ministry, and the calling of the disciples to form a new community made up of Jews and Gentiles that will fulfil Israel's calling. We shall examine each of these four aspects of the foundations of a new world order, for a new order is what Jesus is establishing (see Ephesians 2:11–22), thus bringing about all that was promised in the Old Testament.

The baptism of Christ

In Matthew's account, Jesus arrives dramatically at the waters of Jordan even as his coming is announced by the preaching of his cousin, John. The Baptist says:

> ". . . after me will come one who is more powerful than I, whose sandals I am not fit to carry. He will baptize you with the Holy Spirit and with fire. His winnowing fork is in his hand, and he will clear his threshing floor, gathering wheat into his barn and burning up the chaff with unquenchable fire."
>
> *Matthew 3:11–12*

It is a picture of power and judgement, purity and cleansing. As soon as John has finished speaking, Jesus is at the bank of the Jordan seeking baptism himself, although John tries to deter him.

The problem John faces in baptizing Jesus is not initially spelled out, but it soon becomes clear. John's baptism is one of repentance. John says that he baptizes with water 'for repentance' (3:11), yet Jesus has no sin for which he needs to repent. He is, after all, the sinless Son of God, yet he comes to John who is administering a baptism of repentance. Why? Jesus understands John's reluctance to baptize him, for when John later says, "I need to be baptized by you, and do you come to me?" (3:14), Jesus replies, "Let it be so now; it is proper for us to do this to fulfil all righteousness" (3:15). What is this *righteousness* that Jesus is fulfilling? Presumably it is the will of his Father that Jesus immerses himself in identification with all those who want a new beginning in their spiritual lives. R. T. France comments that as Jesus is baptized with others at the Jordan:

> . . . he is identified with all those who by accepting John's baptism have declared their desire for a new beginning with God. He thus prepares for his own role in 'bearing their weaknesses' (8:17) and eventually 'giving his life as a ransom for many' (20:28) through shedding his blood for their forgiveness (26:28). If he is to be their representative, he must first be identified with them.[25]

Like an army commander who shares his troops' discomfort, though he has no need to, Jesus steps into the waters of the Jordan to identify with those he has come to lead and save, although personally he has no need of baptism.

The second event that occurs at his baptism is that Jesus, in the very act of immersing himself in the task he has come to embrace, is equipped with the divine power to accomplish it. The Spirit comes upon him. The descent of the Spirit on the Messiah fulfils several messianic prophecies of Isaiah (Isaiah 11:2; 42:1; 61:1). The one who is to baptize with the Spirit is himself baptized or filled by the same Spirit. The resulting combination of the Son of God with the Spirit of God is the necessary partnership for fulfilling the mission of God. As one of the great Early Church Fathers,

Gregory of Nyssa, wrote in the fourth century when defending the divinity of the Son and the Spirit:

> All that the Father is, we see revealed in the Son; all that is the Son's is the Father's also; for the whole Son dwells in the Father, and he has the whole Father dwelling in himself . . . The Son who exists always in the Father can never be separated from him, nor can the Spirit ever be divided from the Son who through the Spirit works all things. He who receives the Father also receives at the same time the Son and the Spirit.[26]

The Spirit comes upon Jesus in visible form. As soon as he comes up out of the water, heaven is opened and the Spirit descends upon Jesus like a dove (3:16). The sign of a dove, chosen to indicate the Spirit's presence, symbolizes peace, salvation and hope, as in the case of the dove released by Noah at the end of the flood (Genesis 8:8–12). In Noah's story the dove brings hope for the end of the flood and a new beginning. Likewise Jesus' ministry in the power of the Spirit brings hope of a new beginning, peace and salvation.

The final "action" that occurs during the baptism of Jesus is the Father speaking words of affirmation and reassurance. In the Gospels there are just three recorded instances of a voice speaking from heaven: at the baptism of Christ (Matthew 3:17; Mark 1:11; Luke 3:22), the transfiguration (Matthew 17:5; Mark 9:7; Luke 9:35), and before the Passion (John 12:28). Each time the voice of the Father either affirms Jesus as his beloved Son, to whom humans should listen, or assures the hearers that he (the Father) will glorify his name in the Son. At the outset of Jesus' ministry, the Father speaks of him as his beloved Son: "This is my Son, whom I love; with him I am well pleased" (3:17). This declaration of love echoes the words of Isaiah 42:1, where the prophet says of the Servant, "Here is my servant, whom I uphold, my chosen one, in whom my soul takes pleasure". It also echoes God's words to Abraham about Isaac, when God says, "Take your son, your only son Isaac, whom you love, and go to the region of Moriah. Sacrifice him there . . ." (Genesis 22:2). In the light of these Old Testament phrases, the words of affirmation at the baptism not only affirm the Father's love for Jesus, but also initiate the inevitable journey to Golgotha (like Mount Moriah), where the beloved Son will offer himself as a sacrifice for the world. Despite these overtones of sacrifice and the echo of the "Servant Songs" in Isaiah, the words in themselves must have brought deep assurance to Jesus, shortly before that assurance would be fiercely tested.

The baptism of Jesus amounts to a foundation stone in his ministry. He graciously identifies with humanity, seeking to find a new way forward through the repentance of John's baptism, and so immerses himself in the task ahead (his vocation). He is equipped and empowered by the Spirit, who comes to him in the symbol of a dove, and is assured of his Father's love. For anyone starting a new ministry these things are likewise foundational. A person must have a clear sense of calling; they need to be equipped by the Spirit, and as they set out, be assured of the Father's love. Such blessings do not mean there will not be testing, however, for Jesus was then—amazingly—"led by the Spirit into the desert to be tempted by the devil" (4:1).

The testing of Jesus: the Son of God

As soon as Jesus is baptized, the Spirit actively leads him into the desert to be tested by the devil. Only Luke and Matthew have a full account of the temptation or testing of Jesus in the wilderness (Matthew 4:1–11; Luke 4:1–13). Mark has a much abbreviated version (Mark 1:12,13), although he shows the force of the Spirit by using a Greek word which suggests Jesus being literally "kicked out" into the desert for the temptations.

Once again, Jesus is following the sequence of Israel. Just as Israel went down into Egypt to escape the threat of starvation (Genesis 46:3,4), so Jesus escapes the threats of Herod by his own journey to Egypt. Like Israel, Jesus passes through the waters—not of the Red Sea, but of baptism in the river Jordan. And now, like Israel, Jesus is found in the desert, where his testing is to take place. Jesus' life parallels that of Israel, fulfilling an earlier calling. Furthermore, Jesus responds to the testing he faces in the desert by using quotations or teachings from the book of Deuteronomy (chapters 6—8). Deuteronomy was Moses' great summary of lessons drawn from Israel's forty years of wandering in the wilderness.

The actual temptations are preceded by a period of fasting (4:2). Forty days of fasting once again parallel the forty years of Israel's wanderings in the wilderness. And it is when Jesus is at his most vulnerable, after a heroic fast similar to Moses' fast on Sinai (Exodus 34:28; Deuteronomy 9:9), that the tempter comes to him. The word "comes" has here the sense of coming to worship ("*proskuneo*") and is frequently used in Matthew's Gospel of those who come to Jesus recognizing his majesty. However, in the case of the tempter, such an approach would have been only a form of make-believe, for soon Satan's real purpose is revealed.

The three temptations are essentially attacks on the person and the calling of Jesus as the Son of God. Each of the tempter's attacks is presaged with the little word "if". Two are invitations to Jesus to prove he is the Son of God; the third is a more blatant attempt by the devil to gain pre-eminent power through the unthinkable event of Jesus giving him his worship.

The first temptation plays on Jesus' acute physical hunger as a human being, following his forty-day fast, and also on his knowledge that he has the divine power to satisfy that hunger by performing a selfish miracle. More than that, says the tempter, it would be a way Jesus can prove to himself that he really is the Son of God. Thus the devil begins by insinuating the thought (using the word "if") that Jesus may not truly be the Son of God and needs to prove it to himself by converting stones to bread. This will have the double effect of staunching his hunger after a forty-day fast and at the same time proving he is the Son of God. Yet Jesus has no need to prove his own standing as God's Son, nor will he use his divine power to satisfy his own hunger. He responds by using a text from Deuteronomy 8:3, quoting Moses telling the Israelites that "one does not live by bread alone, but by every word that comes from the mouth of God" (4:4, NRSV).

The second temptation appears to be not only a further opportunity for Jesus to prove he is the Son of God, but also a way of forcing the Father to protect the Son from harm, "as if God is there to serve his Son, rather than the reverse".[27] Jumping from the highest pinnacle of the temple in full public view would not only be a stunt, but it would force the Father's hand to save the Son from ignominy. The devil gives further plausibility to his temptation by assuring the Son of his safety, should he throw himself from the pinnacle of the temple, by using a quotation from Psalm 91:11–12, in which angels are promised to protect him (4:6). Jesus replies that the whole scheme is an uncalled-for test of God the Father, once again quoting from Deuteronomy (6:16), using the words that reprove Israel for putting God to the test at Massah (Exodus 17:7). The very idea of the Father having to rescue Jesus, catching him as he falls to the ground from the pinnacle of the temple, in fact demonstrates a lack of trust, because it would force the Father to prove his love following a ridiculous prank.

If the first temptation represents a misuse of power, and the second an abuse of trust, the third temptation is the most blatant and crude appeal to Jesus to change allegiance and gain short-term power, without integrity or suffering. Jesus is taken to a high mountain from which he can see the kingdoms of the world, which suggests the temptation takes the form of a vision (4:8). With extraordinary temerity and arrogant brashness, the devil offers all the kingdoms of the world to Jesus, if he will only bow down and worship him. With words from Deuteronomy 6:13, Jesus dismisses Satan, using the tempter's fallen angelic name, and saying, "Away from me, Satan! For it is written: 'Worship the Lord your God, and serve him only.'" It is such an emphatic reply to what is the most far-reaching temptation that could have been lain before Jesus, that there is nothing more the malevolent tempter can do.

What the devil offers is power without integrity, corruption without hope of redemption, and glory of the shabbiest kind, with no cost. Jesus will be exalted to the highest place by his Father after the cross and resurrection; he will be given the name that is above every name, will have all authority, and all will indeed bow to him (Philippians 2:9–11; Matthew 28:18), but only after fulfilling his calling in which he gives his life as "a sacrifice of atonement" (Romans 3:25). Flatly and firmly rejected, the devil slinks off and waits for a more opportune time when Jesus will again be vulnerable (see Luke 4:13; Matthew 26:36–44).

Jesus' testing and temptations are now at an end, at least for the time being. A Spirit-led encounter with his arch-enemy leaves Jesus exhausted, and he is ministered to by angels (4:11). He is nevertheless battle-hardened, ready and strengthened for what lies ahead. No disciple following in the footsteps of Jesus can avoid testing and temptation. A disciple cannot always dwell in green pastures—the rugged pathway invariably calls, requiring both endurance and faithfulness. The testing can be in the circumstances and challenges of life: disappointments and losses sometimes crowd in, or we may find ourselves in the deepest water, needing to find Christ's grace and strength. Alternatively, our temptations can simply lure us into actions that are damaging to our faith, to others or to ourselves. Such temptations might include a wrong relationship, not fulfilling our vows to another, or entering into a shady deal or conspiracy against another in order to improve our chances of success. All such temptations have behind them, and in them, the seedy machinations of Satan. They need to be resisted by the sword of the Spirit, which is the word of God. In this way the disciple follows the peerless example of the Lord.

The beginnings of ministry

Having been baptized, with all that meant, and having faced the testing of the devil, Jesus now begins his ministry. John's Gospel suggests that Jesus spends some time in the vicinity of the Jordan baptizing, before returning to Nazareth once John the Baptist is arrested (John 3:22,26; Matthew 4:12). Jesus then goes to Nazareth in Galilee where, Luke tells us, he gives his opening sermon (Luke 4:14–30). He makes his base at Capernaum for his Galilean ministry around the lake, further fulfilling the prophecy of scripture (Matthew 4:13–16). Galilee is to be the place from whence Jesus' mission is launched and developed and, following his resurrection, from here the mission of the kingdom will be relaunched (Matthew 28:10; John 2:1–12). Typically, Matthew quotes from Isaiah:

> Land of Zebulun and land of Naphtali,
> the way to the sea, along the Jordan,
> Galilee of the Gentiles –
> the people living in darkness
> have seen a great light;
> on those living in the land of the shadow of death
> a light has dawned.
>
> *Matthew 4:15–16 (cf. Isaiah 9:1–2)*

The quotation is closer to the original Hebrew than the Greek translation of the Hebrew Scriptures called the Septuagint, and thereby shows Matthew's familiarity with the Hebrew text.[28] The quotation tells us that Jesus will first proclaim the kingdom in the land of Zebulun and in the land of Naphtali.[29] It is in their territory that the radiance of the Son of God will shine, giving light to those who live in darkness and under the shadow of death. It is here that Jesus will make a beginning, as prophesied by Isaiah. Galilee as a region has many attractions: it is not Jerusalem, nor is it the religious hothouse of Judea; it is open to Gentile influence and presence; it contains many unpretentious ordinary folk; it is a place from which many Jewish hotheads and revolutionaries come and so is used to someone unusual breaking new ground. So it is in this area, chosen by God hundreds of years before, that the kingdom is to be announced by the humble, hidden king. As Matthew writes, "From that time on Jesus began to preach, 'Repent, for the kingdom of heaven is near.'" (4:17).

Many commentators see this as the beginning of the next major section of the Gospel, in which the Messiah is revealed in word and deed. The final section of the Gospel begins with a similar formula ("From that time on . . .") after Peter's identification of Jesus as the Messiah: "From that time on Jesus began to explain to his disciples that he must go to Jerusalem and suffer many things at the hands of the elders, chief priests and teachers of the law, and that he must be killed and on the third day be raised to life." (16:21).

Between these two literary formulae of "From that time on", Jesus reveals who he is, firstly through his preaching in word and deed, and then, secondly, through the extraordinary and unique mission of his death and resurrection. At the same time, he begins to gather a community of disciples who will carry on the ministry when he has completed his work on earth.

The founding of a new community

In just a few verses, which seem to be sandwiched between the exciting beginnings of Jesus' ministry, we find the calling of some of the first disciples: Simon, later called Peter, and his brother Andrew, then James and John the sons of Zebedee (4:18–22). They will form the basis of the new community which Jesus will draw together. Three of these disciples make up the core of Jesus' followers who are with him at many of the critical moments of his ministry: the raising of Jairus' daughter, the transfiguration and the agony in the Garden of Gethsemane. Yet it is easy to overlook the immensity of what takes place.

It may just seem initially like the calling of two sets of brothers, but it is in fact the laying of the first foundation stones in a new global community that will eventually fill the earth and heavens, and be the fulfilment of God's mysterious plan for the universe. To get the full flavour of this we must take Paul as our guide. In the second chapter of his Epistle to the Ephesians he states:

> . . . you [Ephesian Christians, and indeed all Christians] are no longer foreigners and aliens, but fellow-citizens with God's people and members of God's household, built on the foundation of the apostles and prophets, with Christ Jesus himself as the chief cornerstone.
>
> *Ephesians 2:19–20*

Here is the beginning of this building, and the laying of the foundation stones of Peter and the other apostles. Who would have known that the call of Jesus to these fishermen beside Galilee was to lay the foundations of this new community? Unlike most rabbis, Jesus does not wait for his followers to choose to follow him as their teacher; instead, he *calls* them to leave their occupations, their family homes, their family members and—in the end—their country. Such is Jesus' charisma and authority that they obey. With a wordplay on their profession, he promises to make them "fishers of people" (4:19). Simon Peter and Andrew are casting their nets beside their boat. James and John are preparing or mending their nets, intent on fishing, but both sets of brothers *leave* their nets to follow. It may have been just a little earlier that Peter, Andrew, James and John have witnessed the great catch of fish recorded in Luke 5, which would have given them more of a miraculous basis for their decision to follow. In any event, with either much or little evidence at this point as to the identity of Jesus, they embark on *the* adventure of their lives, from which they will never again return to the normality of fishing, apart from briefly after the resurrection (John 21), and which will transform them for ever.

The summary of Jesus' ministry

The final section of this foundation-laying chapter is a summary of the ministry of Jesus in Galilee. After he makes Capernaum his base, Matthew tells us that Jesus goes throughout Galilee doing three things: teaching in the synagogues, preaching the good news of the kingdom, and healing every disease and sickness (4:23). These three actions form the core of his activity; they are the verbs of his life. They make a triad of which Matthew is especially fond, and will frequently form a trope or motif in his Gospel.

Jesus' teaching takes place in synagogues: small places of worship for local communities, found in most towns and villages. It is here that people receive their instruction and that community life is nurtured, but it is also here that Jesus finds both opposition and hypocrisy. Indeed, the dynamic of instruction, opposition and hypocrisy is often found in Matthew's Gospel, and these things are frequently exposed by the ministry of Jesus in the synagogues.

Speaking in the synagogue provides Jesus with an opportunity to teach from the Scriptures, which are read systematically during Sabbath worship. He preaches in a way that challenges his hearers to the core (see Mark 1:21–28; Luke 4:14–30) and throws startling new light on the Scriptures. In these instances of instruction, in both Mark and Luke, Jesus' teaching leads to action, such as the deliverance of a man from an evil spirit (Mark 1:23–26). Sometimes it leads him to say that Old Testament prophecies are being fulfilled in him (Luke 4:14–30). In any event, Jesus' teaching in the synagogues is a distinctive part of his ministry. Furthermore, for Matthew, teaching is instrumental in the transformation Jesus is bringing.

Secondly, Jesus preaches "the good news of the kingdom" (4:23). This is the second time the kingdom is mentioned (here Matthew does not use the phrase "the kingdom of God" or the "kingdom of heaven", which is his preference, but simply "the kingdom"). The phrase the "good news of the kingdom" is best understood as the good news of God's reigning or ruling.[30] Kingdom, in that sense, is a "verb-noun", or a noun that is "doing". What it is doing is bringing about the presence of God's rule, indeed the "presence of the future", as George Eldon Ladd coined it in his book of that name. So in what Jesus teaches or preaches and in the healing that he brings, he is demonstrating the nature of God's rule. This kingdom is good news, *"euangelion"*, a word that Matthew uses only sparingly in his Gospel (see 9:35; 24:14; 26:13). Jesus preaches or announces the good news and proclaims that with him, the rule of God is being made known.

Alongside the preaching or announcement of the presence of the kingdom, the final part of the triad of teaching, preaching and healing—and the one that makes this rule abundantly clear—is healing. Words instruct and announce, but healing demonstrates what the words proclaim, and includes deliverance from evil. It is total healing: every disease and sickness is included. Matthew means that every disease and sickness brought to Jesus is healed, not that every disease in the region is cured.

In the next verse (4:24) Matthew makes this plain. Jesus' fame spreads beyond the borders of Israel into Syria, the neighbouring province. Indeed, the whole region comes under the Provincial Roman Governor of Syria based in Antioch, which is one of three great provincial capitals outside Rome (the others are Carthage and Alexandria). Galilee and the Decapolis, the ten cities in the north of Palestine, and either side of the Jordan, are to become the main areas of Jesus' ministry north of Judea, Jerusalem and Perea. In Matthew's Gospel, tellingly, no mention is made of Samaria or of Jesus' ministry among the Samaritans (unlike John 4:1–42 or Luke 9:51–56). Perhaps Matthew thinks it will be too controversial for the Jews if he makes reference to Jesus' inclusion of the Samaritans. Such are the Jewish prejudices against Samaritans that any mention of them in connection with Jesus might prevent Jews from seriously considering his claims.

By the end of this opening section, in which the foundations of Jesus' ministry are laid, Jesus is followed by "large crowds" (4:25) drawn from the whole region. His ministry now begins to unfold. Having been equipped in his baptism at the outset, and then tested fiercely by the devil, Jesus truly begins his ministry, in which he proclaims the rule or kingdom of heaven through the triple activity of teaching, preaching and healing. It is also the moment when Matthew assembles the longest account of Jesus' teaching, which we shall call his "teaching on discipleship in the new community", although it is more commonly known as the "Sermon on the Mount".

CHAPTER 3

Fulfilling the Calling of a Disciple

There are two main teaching themes in the Sermon on the Mount: the first is instruction about the attitudes and spiritual disciplines of the disciple, and the second is about Jesus' extension and fulfilment of the law. The Sermon on the Mount is one of a number of discourses in Matthew, and surely the most famous. It is not so much a universal ethical teaching for humankind, as is often supposed, but rather a charter for the disciple.

It is, most probably, a gathering together of Jesus' teaching on discipleship. "All this suggests that these chapters do not represent a single actual sermon" but "a collection of Jesus' teaching bearing in different ways on the theme of discipleship," says R. T. France.[31] The Sermon answers the questions "How are we to follow Jesus?" and "How does Jesus fulfil the law?" The answers given in the Sermon are comprehensive, demanding and radical. In this chapter we shall look at the attitudes, activities and blessings of the disciple.

The Beatitudes

The search for happiness is one of the great human quests. The United States Declaration of Independence drafted by Thomas Jefferson says:

> We hold these truths to be sacred and undeniable; that all [people] are created equal and independent, that from that equal creation they derive rights inherent and inalienable, among which are the preservation of life, and liberty, and the pursuit of happiness.

It is a majestic and laudable statement. The greatest minds, from Plato to Cicero, or from Hobbes to Lyotard, have sought to understand ways human beings might be happy. To be happy is a reasonable human ambition, but how to achieve it is unclear. Too often happiness is snatched away by our frail human weaknesses. In a radio programme called *Great Lives*, the presenter Matthew Parris and his guest Len Goodman recalled the popularity of songwriter Lionel Bart, the brilliant composer and lyricist of the musical *Oliver!* and of many popular songs. Bart hummed the tunes while others wrote down the music. Despite his success, a mixture of alcohol, bankruptcy, and fear that his homosexuality would be exposed robbed him of happiness. He could write the song "Where is Love?" for *Oliver!*, but how to find love himself? The Beatitudes (or, if we divide the word into its components, the *be-attitudes*) are Jesus' statement about those attitudes which make us blessed or happy. They are not a hedonist's charter, nor do they advocate the pursuit of self-interest. Instead they follow the teaching of Jesus in this vital respect: if we want to find our life, we must lose it (Matthew 10:39).

Beatitudes are found in many different cultures besides Judaism and Christianity. They are sayings that encapsulate how a person might find happiness. Among Old Testament examples, most notably in Psalm 1, we find the following:

> Happy are those who do not follow the advice of the wicked,
> or take the path that sinners tread, or sit in the seat of scoffers;
> but their delight is in the law of the LORD,
> and on his law they meditate day and night.
> They are like trees planted by streams of water,
> which yield their fruit in its season,
> and their leaves do not wither.
> In all that they do, they prosper.
>
> *Psalm 1:1–3 (NRSV)*

Other Psalms (such as 32:1–2; 40:4; 119:1–3; 128:1) follow suit. Beatitudes are paradoxical, in that the behaviour they call for is often spurned by the world, yet is greatly rewarded in God's economy of blessing. The Beatitudes "call on those who would be God's people to stand out as different from those around them, and promise them that those who do so will not ultimately be the losers."[32] Although God is not mentioned in the giving of rewards, it is implied that it is he who will comfort, give inheritance to, satisfy, show mercy to, and call his children those who are thus blessed.

In Jesus' day, beatitudes had taken on a particular form established as part of a Rabbi's or teacher's repertoire, but here Jesus gives them sharpness and memorability, as well as a vivid, paradoxical character that takes them to a new level (5:3–12). The opening word "blessed", from which we get the general name "beatitude" (the Latin "*beati sunt*" means "blessed are"), is a translation of *makarios*", which later comes to be a term of address in the Orthodox Church. "*Makarios*" "does not denote one whom God blesses"[33] as much as one who is fortunate, translating the Hebrew "*ašrê*". The sense is, therefore, that the person whose life is characterized by the quality described will have a particular reward.

Thus the opening of Matthew's eight Beatitudes says, "Blessed are the poor in spirit, for theirs is the kingdom of heaven" (5:3). The paradoxical nature of this teaching is immediately laid bare: the poor in spirit are rewarded with nothing less than membership of the kingdom. What is being extolled here is not material poverty, as if that were a blessing in itself, but rather a humble dependence on God for all things. The poor or weak are frequently praised in the Old Testament (see, for example, Isaiah 61:1–2; Psalm 37:11). Moses was praised for being the meekest or most humble man in all the earth (Numbers 12:3). This emphasis on meekness or poverty of spirit is nothing if not counter-cultural in the context of the Roman Empire. In that Empire, qualities of ambition, breeding, physical strength, and literary and cultural awareness were all highly prized. Poverty of spirit, leading to dependence on a sovereign and righteous God, was not rated. Indeed, later both historian Edward Gibbon and philosopher Friedrich Nietzsche (in the eighteenth and nineteenth centuries respectively) would express doubt about the Christian virtue of humility, considering that it exchanges power for weakness and was an eventual cause of the decline and fall of the Empire. Yet in the Beatitudes it is the other way round, reflecting Paul's claim, "When I am weak, then I am strong" (2 Corinthians 12:10). Jesus teaches that the kingdom of God, an everlasting and enduring kingdom, is the reward for those who are poor in spirit—that is, people who do not see themselves as intrinsically powerful.

The paradoxical nature of the Beatitudes continues and, if anything, is sharpened further: "Blessed are those who mourn, for they will be comforted" (5:4). It is not that bereavement is blessed in itself, but simply that no form of grieving for that which is just, good or edifying will be overlooked or forgotten. There will be a balm for righteous grieving. Old Testament statements to this effect include "Those who sow with tears will reap with songs of joy" (Psalm 126:5), and that God will "comfort all who mourn, and provide for those who grieve in Zion," giving them "a crown of beauty instead of ashes, the oil of joy instead of mourning" (Isaiah 61:2–3).

I know a couple who suffered years of anxiety, seeing their son's health deteriorate because of aggressive brain tumours which eventually took his life. I have also seen that couple holding a new-born second child in whom they could rejoice, but without such anxiety for the future. Nothing could make up for the loss of their elder child, but there is comfort in their pain. Even if there is no clear ending to grief, or if—at the very least—a heavy heart remains, God is not so unjust as to be indifferent to loss and pain, but will comfort and console. However, sometimes we can only keep silence in the face of another's grief (see the story of Job).

I remember attending a service commemorating road traffic victims at which I spoke, following a terrible crash in our parish. As we walked from the City Hall to lay wreaths at a memorial, I talked to one middle-aged couple, only to discover that *both* their sons had been killed in road crashes (the term preferred to "accidents"). In the face of such loss, sympathy, prayer and even words themselves seem so inadequate. How can anyone experiencing such grief be described as fortunate or blessed?

Nevertheless, comfort can come in the most unexpected ways. A woman who lost her haemophiliac son through an HIV-infected blood transfusion described her devastation on a BBC Radio 4 programme called *The Reunion*. She went home to her bedroom in a state of shock on the day of her son's death, only to see a butterfly come and settle near her on her bed—she felt comforted. Equally, the couple who lost their son, aged only four, from brain tumours were comforted by a rainbow in the sky the evening of his death. These are not explanations, but are forms of comfort beyond words.

Thirdly, Jesus says, "Blessed are the meek, for they will inherit the earth" (or "land"; 5:5). Once again, the characteristic praised here is meekness or poverty of spirit, which translates the Hebrew word "*nāwîm*", used of the meek in the Psalms (as in Psalm 37:11).[34] This word approximates to "humility": one of the primary characteristics of the disciple and godly person. Of humility, Augustine of Hippo said:

> Construct no other way for yourself of grasping and holding
> the truth than the way constructed by Him who, as God, saw
> how faltering were our steps. This way is first, humility, second,
> humility, third, humility.[35]

The reward of the meek is to inherit the land: in other words, to enjoy a reversal of fortunes. Those who do not grasp for anything will be rewarded.

Generally, in biblical hermeneutics or interpretation, Old Testament promises about the land have a non-territorial fulfilment in the New Testament. In his work *The Gospel and the Land*, W. D. Davies argues that for Matthew, "'inheriting the land' is synonymous with entering the Kingdom and . . . this Kingdom transcends all geographic dimensions and is spiritualized."[36] If this is correct, Jesus teaches that it is the poor in spirit, those who are not self-regarding, who are likely to enter the kingdom of heaven, as in the Parable of the Pharisee and the Tax Collector (Luke 18:9–14).

The fourth Beatitude breaks new ground: "Blessed are those who hunger and thirst for righteousness, for they will be filled" (5:6). The key concept here is righteousness or "*dikaiosyne*". In the Septuagint, this Greek word translates the Hebrew "*tzedakah*", often rendered by the words "deliverance" or "salvation". However, the sense of this Beatitude is best captured by the paraphrase, "Blessed are those who hunger and thirst *to see right prevail*," as the New English Bible has it. In other words, these are the kinds of people who long for justice and for vindication of the righteous. They are the kinds of people who look around the world and want to see the triumph of right conduct, fair play and good values, but more especially want to exhibit these in their own lives. People who make it their ambition to live in this manner will find God their eager partner. In the same way, Jesus said to his disciples, "My food is to do the will of him who sent me and to finish his work" (John 4:34). God will fill people who have this desire; literally, they will be "stuffed"—a Greek word used for the fattening of animals! The language serves to confirm God's longing for justice on earth and his desire to work generously with all those who have the same desire, for themselves and for others.

The fifth Beatitude, "Blessed are the merciful, for they will be shown mercy" (5:7), recalls the words spoken by Portia to Shylock in Shakespeare's *The Merchant of Venice*:

> The quality of mercy is not strain'd,
> It droppeth as the gentle rain from heaven
> Upon the place beneath: it is twice blest;
> It blesseth him that gives and him that takes:
> 'Tis mightiest in the mightiest: it becomes
> The throned monarch better than his crown . . .[37]

Mercy here is not only the willingness to forgive, but also to adopt a generous attitude more generally, in which we see things from another's point of view. Mercy is not quick to take offence or gloat over others' shortcomings. Such mercy calls forth God's mercy, in the same way that in knowing God's forgiveness we forgive others too. Mercy and forgiveness have reciprocal power. If we are forgiven, then we forgive, and if we are shown mercy, we too should show mercy.

The sixth Beatitude, "Blessed are the pure in heart, for they will see God" (5:8), involves the heart or lens of our being. Just as dirty glasses obscure the clarity of our sight, so a soiled heart obscures the clarity of our spiritual vision of God. In Psalm 24, the Psalmist says it is the person who has "clean hands and a pure heart" who can "ascend the hill of the Lord"; likewise it is the person of integrity who longs for God's presence who will see clearly and be rewarded with a still clearer vision of God in the face of Jesus Christ (Psalm 24:3–6; 2 Corinthians 4:6).

The seventh Beatitude is about peacemaking: "Blessed are the peacemakers, for they will be called sons of God" (5:9). God, in Jesus Christ, is the supreme peacemaker. Paul tells us Christ made peace by the blood of his cross, for "he himself is our peace, who has made the two groups [Jews and Gentiles] one and has destroyed the barrier, the dividing wall of hostility" (Ephesians 2:14) by tearing it down. Human beings build walls; God loves to tear them down. As a boy I lived in the city of Berlin, where my father was in the military. As we arrived in the city, in August 1961, the East German government built the Berlin Wall with support from the Soviet Union. It would remain in place until 1989, when it was demolished and the two sides of the city were reunited. Disciples of Christ are called to be peacemakers, joining in the work of tearing down the walls of suspicion, prejudice, hatred and hostility, in order that all might be one under Christ. Those who get involved in the work of peacemaking will rightly be called sons or children of God. They will resemble their Father in heaven.

The last and eighth Beatitude brings to mind the suffering Church and those who are persecuted. "Blessed are those who are persecuted because of righteousness, for theirs is the kingdom of heaven," says Jesus (5:10). It is not that persecution is a blessing, but rather that in persecution disciples may *find* blessing—that is, God's presence, favour and encouragement. There is no doubt that in the last century Christians faced more persecution than in any century since the founding of the Church. In Russia after the Revolution, literally thousands of priests, ministers and ordinary Christian people were punished in prison camps or with death. Likewise the Church in China and in North Korea has been systematically persecuted, and now, in the Middle East, in Pakistan, and even in India, Christians face formidable persecution; churches, whether in Iraq or Syria, are being wiped out, with the Copts in Egypt facing persistent violence and persecution. The promise of Jesus is that in these circumstances, Christians will be rewarded by being the epicentre of the kingdom of heaven, much like the poor in spirit. Or, as one of the elders says in the book of Revelation:

> "These are they who have come out of the great tribulation; they have washed their robes and made them white in the blood of the Lamb. Therefore, they are before the throne of God and serve him day and night in his temple . . ."
>
> *Revelation 7:14–15a*

This concludes the eight Beatitudes of Jesus. In fact, the reward of the poor in spirit and the reward of those who are persecuted ("for theirs is the kingdom of heaven") form an "*inclusio*", a literary device whereby a piece of teaching is bracketed within a repeated formula. Often, in the Psalms, David begins and ends with "Happy" or "Blessed is the one . . ." Jesus not only uses the formula of beatitude, but gives it a rabbinical structure with this *inclusio* device.

The final blessing for those who are insulted or persecuted for their faith (5:11–12) is in many ways an amplification of the eighth Beatitude. Despite such treatment, they are to rejoice. Early Christians such as Ignatius, Bishop of Antioch and Perpetua of Carthage fulfilled this command completely: they went rejoicing to their martyrdom!

Jesus now makes two general statements about the effect of this new community of disciples that he is forming: "You (plural) are the salt of the earth," and "You are the light of the world" (5:13–14). The vocation to be salt and light is a great one. Salt preserves, cleanses and brings taste; light illuminates darkness, therefore it guides and enlightens. Yet the effectiveness of both can be impaired: salt may be kept in the salt cellar and so be of no use, and light can be hidden under a bowl and give off no rays of illumination. Salt needs to be in use to preserve meat and fish, to enhance taste, and be applied as an antiseptic; likewise light must be cast by a lamp in order to illuminate a room. Disciples must not keep their faith to themselves but must spread it in society, shining their light in visible ways. If they fail to do these things, their saltiness will be of no value and their light will remain hidden.

In the next chapter we will look at Jesus' teaching about the law, which forms an important part of the Sermon on the Mount, but first we explore the five broad ways in which discipleship is truly formed.

The spiritual disciplines of true discipleship

What are the spiritual disciplines of discipleship? If the Beatitudes show the kind of *attitudes* Jesus extols, he now turns his attention to commonly accepted areas of personal *discipleship*: behaviour relating to giving and possessions, prayer and fasting, food and clothing, and relationships with others. At the time it was the Pharisees who provided the commonly accepted model of spirituality, and it is in contradistinction to this model that Jesus now teaches, offering a model of discipleship which is very different from theirs.

Jesus begins by teaching about almsgiving or what we might call charitable giving, whether to individuals or organizations (6:1–4). In his day, there was no social security or healthcare, and it was the charity of neighbours that prevented people from falling into abject poverty or helped them in times of crisis. Nevertheless, as we know from the Gospel stories, there were still many beggars who relied on the handouts of passers-by to keep them from starvation. Jesus' teaching about giving is mainly about *how* it is done.

As with fasting and prayer, it is assumed that people will give. Hence Jesus says not, "If you give," but rather, "When you give". The main thrust of what Jesus is teaching is that people should not look for earthly reward for their "acts of righteousness", but rather give secretly, having their reward in heaven. There is to be no show or ostentation in giving, nor any imitation of the hypocrites who love to make a song and dance about their giving by announcing it with a trumpet blast; rather, it must be done *secretly* (without the left hand knowing what the right hand is doing) and the reward from our heavenly Father will likewise be in secret. The underlying principle is that *the way* we give is as important as *what* we give.

Furthermore, Jesus provides additional instruction about a disciple's attitude to wealth (Matthew 6:19–24). He states that accumulation of spiritual investments and wealth in heaven are more important than the accumulation of goods and wealth on earth. Once more Jesus is at home in the dichotomy between earth and heaven: two realities in which the ephemeral nature of earth is overtaken by the permanence of heaven. Not only that, but the imperative of heaven succeeding earth means that the disciple's eye and will (6:22–24) must be continually cleansed by an assessment of priorities, and by asking such questions as "What is of lasting value?" "What way of life is truly healthy?" "What is the right perspective on living?" Answering these questions honestly reorientates the disciple's life, so that no false assumptions are made and life is lived with an eternal perspective rather than with a focus on accumulating wealth for selfish ends. What seems permanent here can so easily turn out to be passing, because corruption, theft or decay can swiftly eat into what has been accumulated on earth.

Along with his teaching on possessions Jesus covers the subjects of prayer and fasting (6:5–18). The teaching on prayer includes, as with giving, an exhortation to secrecy and simplicity. Once again Jesus' teaching is in sharp contrast to the way in which the Pharisees, the spiritual authorities of Jesus' day, pray. They are play-actors or hypocrites and they love to pray ostentatiously in public (6:5), turning prayer into a performance made impressive by many words and pious gestures. According to Jesus, this does not impress his heavenly Father. The Pharisees' reward is in the misplaced admiration of the populace for their hollow spirituality, which will in time be revealed for what it is. Jesus teaches his disciples both *how* to pray and *what* to pray in a pattern of praying we call the Lord's Prayer.

Firstly, as with almsgiving, prayer must not be done publicly for the praise of others, but in secret. Jesus' disciples should go into a private space and pray there and "your Father, who sees what is done in secret, will reward you" (6:6). Likewise, prayer is not heard for its many words, but for its simplicity, honesty and faith (6:7). These are the values Jesus seeks to establish in our praying, not showiness or self-serving piety, or desire for human applause. Instead, simplicity and secrecy seem to be the hallmarks of the style of praying Jesus commends.

Jesus goes on to give his disciples a model prayer which has come to be known simply as the Lord's Prayer (6:9–13). Along with the Ten Commandments, it has been a pillar of the spirituality of the Church from earliest times, often written up on either side of the east end communion table in parish churches. The function of the prayer seems to be at least threefold: it can be prayed as it stands (and this is the case with most liturgies that include it); it is a template for more extended prayer, with its clauses functioning as headings for different aspects of our praying; and lastly, it can be the basis for instruction on prayer. The fact that the Lord's Prayer appears in slightly different forms in the Gospels (see Luke 11:2–4) shows that the Early Church was not precious about saying the words in precisely the same way. Instead, the phrases encapsulate the attitudes and expectations that Jesus is looking for in prayer.

The Lord's Prayer can be divided into two parts, each with three clauses. Significantly, the prayer is addressed to God as "Father" ("*Abba*"), which is the Christians' name for God and the name Jesus uses to address the Almighty. The first part of the prayer is to do with our approach to God: his name (or being) is to be honoured or revered; his kingdom is to come, and his will is to be done on earth as in heaven. Each of these petitions begins with the word "may"– "May your name be held in awe, may your kingdom come, and may your will be done, as in heaven so also on earth." These petitions align our perspective and desires with our heavenly Father's. We appreciate his glory, long for his kingdom and submit to his will. After beginning our prayer in this way, we are ready to make further petitions, which likewise follow three themes. These themes are our daily needs (literally, "bread for today and tomorrow") or as Origen puts it, "our needful bread";[38] our willingness to forgive reciprocally as we ourselves are forgiven; and lastly, our need for deliverance from future trials or temptations, that we may be neither crushed nor suborned by them. By praying these three petitions we bring our daily needs to our Father for his provision, we keep our relationships with others in good repair by forgiving any hurt caused to us (or, at the very least, by being willing to take the first step on the path to offering forgiveness); and we are kept from being overwhelmed by trials or overtaken by sin. Here is an all-encompassing prayer, setting boundaries to how we should pray, and one which fulfils all prayer in the Old Testament, moving us to the intimacy of a child–father relationship.

After giving us a pattern for praying in the Lord's Prayer, and before explaining the right attitudes towards fasting, Jesus also teaches the right *qualities* to undergird our praying. We have already seen what is important: we should not be ostentatious in praying, but simple and plain, praying in secret rather than grandstanding like the hypocrites. Later, in Matthew 7:7–12, Jesus adds more qualities to cultivate in prayer: expectancy or confidence, and being convinced in advance of God's generosity. Firstly, Jesus says perseverance will be rewarded: "Ask and it will be given to you; seek and you will find; knock and the door will be opened to you" (7:7). He goes on to say that God can be trusted to act generously: "If you, then, though you are evil, know how to give good gifts to your children, how much more will your Father in heaven give good gifts to those who ask him!" (7:11). Perseverance and confidence are important qualities in prayer, although we do not always see the results we hope for: a disease claims the life of a loved one despite much prayer, a job offer does not come, a relationship does not take off, a house will not sell, hopes are disappointed. "Where is the generosity of God?" we cry; "What use is my perseverance now?" Perhaps the generosity of God is that in the midst of any disappointment we may suffer, he does not leave us; he is always present to us and to those we love. His desire is to give us a future and a hope (Jeremiah 29:11).

Jesus teaches in a similar vein on fasting (6:16–18). Once again the emphasis is on not showing ostentatiously that we are fasting. There is to be no disfiguring of the face with ashes, or looking sombre. Instead, unlike the hypocrites of Jesus' time, or indeed some ascetic movements of early Christianity who frowned on clean clothes or baths, the person fasting should conceal that they are abstaining from food or drink.[39] There is a place for fasting and asceticism, but it is not to be turned into theatre. It is to be concealed, so that no hint of pride mars this spiritual discipline that is a true accompaniment to prayer.

Jesus teaches two more spiritual disciplines in the Sermon on the Mount. They are the need to trust our heavenly Father for our welfare, and the need to foster positive relationships with others by not judging or criticizing. Trust in our heavenly Father over matters of food, clothing and health is to replace anxiety (6:25–34). Pick up any newspaper's weekend colour supplement in the UK, and you can almost guarantee that the same subjects will be covered exhaustively, as if we can never hear too much about them: food, slimming, clothes and sex. This is the monotonously regular diet of weekend readers in Britain, and probably over most of the Western world. The reason for its persistence is our fascination with these things which concern our bodies and our image. It is fair to say that bodies and image have become the chief concerns in modern society. Indeed, the constant bombardment with images of unattainable bodies often encourages people to live unhealthy and anxious lives to obtain them. The advertised body might be attainable for a brief period in someone's life, but then the reality of living takes over and causes the wrinkles or weight we so much dread: work, childbearing and rearing, ageing and sickness all take their toll.[40] People sometimes literally die over their image; others might deride it on- or off-line. There is great anxiety relating to appearance and the way others see us, whether on social media or in real life. Jesus was teaching in a society where there was great material scarcity, and hence anxiety about where food or clothing might be found. We, by contrast, live in a society of great material abundance for many, although not for all. Our anxiety is not over the effects of scarcity, but over the effects of abundance, and the hold this projected image of unattainable beauty has on us, in our context of abundant yet stressful living.

Nevertheless, the teaching of Jesus holds true, although for a very different society. We are not to be anxious over our bodies, clothing, diet and health. The call is to trust, as "your heavenly Father" knows what you need; to be like the birds who Martin Luther called "blessed theologians", and the lilies which are more beautiful than all of Solomon's finery (6:28–30). So "do not worry about tomorrow, for tomorrow will worry about itself. Each day has enough trouble of its own" (6:34). This teaching is realistic, sanguine and a challenge to exercise faith, rather than being squeezed into the anxious mould of the world.

The final discipline to which the disciple is called is to refrain from judgement and criticism of others (7:1–5). It is all too easy to fall into proud, censorious or snide judgements; the fact is that criticism of others often makes us feel better about ourselves. Although this is not a call to forgo our critical faculties for the sake of improving what we or others do, it is nevertheless a call to be restrained and circumspect in judging others without undertaking serious reflection on our own shortcomings and weakness. The effect of such self-reflection should be a sober estimation of ourselves and a greater degree of humility. Jesus says the measure of judgement we impose on others will be the measure of judgement we ourselves receive (7:2).

The parable that Jesus uses to caution against criticism of others is taken from the carpenter's workshop, with which he is very familiar, and it is both vivid and humorous. It is far easier to see the speck in another's eye than the great plank in our own; often we have become so accustomed to the great plank in our own eye that we do not notice it, but are nevertheless quick to see the slight imperfection in another. Furthermore, Jesus says disciples must not be hypocrites in their judgement of others, suggesting that such criticism is something to which the disciple is peculiarly prone. Anyone who has been in a church for a while knows that it can be all too easy for one member to criticize or judge another.

Judgemental remarks have a power all their own; once launched they can fester and infect the mind of the recipient. Remarks such as, "You will never be any good;" "You are hopeless;" "You are as thick as two short planks" and so on, can stick, returning again and again, reducing the confidence and potential of a person to naught. The disciple, on the other hand, is supposed to build up, to encourage and to be positive. Equally, precious insights about the faith, which Jesus calls "pearls" (7:6), should not be lightly tossed before those who will neither understand nor appreciate them. Just as the disciple should be circumspect about judging, so he or she should be careful in making spiritual truths known to people prepared only to ridicule them. The wisdom of the cross (see 1 Corinthians 1:18–25) is mocked in the earliest surviving piece of Roman graffiti, in which a Christian, Alexamenos, worships a god depicted as a donkey on a cross. The pagan rulers, for the most part, first ridiculed the faith and then tortured and executed Christians by the score in the "games" across the Empire. What they mocked they then destroyed. Harsh words are too often a preliminarily to something worse.

The teaching that Jesus gives about discipleship covers a wide range of spiritual disciplines: adopting good attitudes, praying and giving, fasting with no hint of ostentation, cultivating a right perspective about material things, trusting for our welfare, not giving in to criticism, and using discretion. This teaching makes up a large proportion of the Sermon on the Mount, Matthew's collection of Jesus' teaching on discipleship. Attentiveness to this teaching will be fruitful, Jesus says. He gives three quick-fire parables to drive the point home: the Parables of the Road, of the Tree, and of the Building (7:13–27). If we follow his teaching, it will ensure we stay on the road that leads to life and not to destruction (7:13–14). If we are grounded in his teaching, we will be like a fruitful tree (7:16–20), and that fruit will be evidence of a true heart. And lastly, if this teaching is not only heard but also put into practice, we will be like a house secured firmly on a rock, able to withstand the storms of life (7:24–27).

From Jesus' teaching on discipleship we turn to his teaching on the law, the other main part of this sermon.

CHAPTER 4

Fulfilment of the Law

The other main theme in the Sermon on the Mount is Jesus as the fulfilment of the law. Matthew is writing for a largely Jewish, early Christian congregation around AD 70–80, quite possibly in the region of Antioch, and one of the questions uppermost in a Jewish Christian's mind would have been the relation of Jesus the Messiah to the law. This is an important theme in Jesus' own teaching to his disciples and to the crowds of his day, as it is in both the mission of the Early Church and in the apostle Paul's teaching, not least in his letters to the Romans and the Galatians.

It is interesting to ponder whether Matthew himself was familiar with the teaching of Paul. Were Paul's letters to the Galatians and the Romans already circulating in the main centres of the Church, for instance? We know that by the end of the first century the Synoptic Gospels (Matthew, Mark, and Luke) were being circulated in Rome, and quite possibly in Antioch, and that the Apostolic Fathers Clement (Bishop of Rome 88–99) and Ignatius (writing around 90–108) knew Paul's letters and were quoting or referring to them in their works.[41] It is therefore quite possible that Matthew, writing from Antioch, knew or had seen some of Paul's epistles. Certainly, Matthew would have known the judgement of the Council of Jerusalem in c.49:

> It seemed good to the Holy Spirit and to us not to burden you with anything beyond the following requirements: You are to abstain from food sacrificed to idols, from blood, from the meat of strangled animals and from sexual immorality. You will do well to avoid these things.
>
> *Acts 15:28–29*

If Matthew had read Paul's letter to the Galatians, written most probably in the late 40s or early 50s after his first missionary journey to that region, he would have seen, "Clearly no-one is justified before God by the law, because, 'The righteous will live by faith'" (Galatians 3:11). Again, Matthew might have read in Paul's letter to the Romans the definitive statement about the gospel and the law: "Therefore no-one will be declared righteous in his sight by observing the law; rather, through the law we become conscious of sin." (Romans 3:20). Of course, we cannot be sure that Matthew *had* read these epistles, but given the frequency with which letters and books were copied in the ancient world, and given that Matthew was probably living in or near the regional city of Antioch, where Paul based himself in the early part of his ministry (Acts 11: 25–26), it would be surprising if Matthew did *not* know the direction of Paul's teaching on the law, especially since Paul was a well-known Pharisee (Philippians 3:4–6), and therefore his views as a Christian would have been very influential.

If we are right to think of the Sermon on the Mount as a compendium of Jesus' teaching, gathered as a body of instruction, a kind of catechesis for a Jewish baptismal candidate, then it is far from surprising to hear Jesus teaching about the law. After all, his relationship with the law would have been uppermost in people's minds. On two occasions Jesus says that both he and his teaching are the fulfilment of the law or, to put it another way, Jesus fulfils all that the law expresses. He fulfils its demands perfectly, pays its penalty on our behalf, and ends our obligation thereto. In other words, Jesus supersedes the law. He is "the end of the law so that there may be righteousness for everyone who believes" (Romans 10:4).

Jesus states categorically that he has not come "to abolish the law or the prophets"; he has "not come to abolish them but to fulfil them" (5:17). A paraphrase of these words is suggested in one commentary: "Far from wanting to set aside the law and the prophets, it is my role to bring into being that to which they have pointed forward, to carry them into a new era of fulfillment."[42] Jesus' fulfilment of the law does not mean that we are free from the searching moral investigation of the law. At the same time, Jesus' fulfilment of the law means that we can now seek justification, or be put right with God, in another way. By expanding the scope of the law into our thoughts and words (not restricting it simply to our actions), as

Jesus does, and by saying that we must obey that deeper demand of the law *perfectly*, he puts entrance into the kingdom on the grounds of perfect obedience to the law beyond our capacity. This is further emphasized by the saying, ". . . unless your righteousness surpasses that of the Pharisees and the teachers of the law, you will certainly not enter the kingdom of heaven" (5:20).

Jesus now shows how the law is to be extended, in this new age, from seemingly only being about our *actions* to being about our *thoughts*, our *feelings* (such as anger) and our *words*. All these aspects of our lives are to be in line with the commandments, not our actions only. In other words, the requirement of the law has become more demanding; the conformity Jesus now looks for is perfection, with the result that no one can be justified by works of the law, for no one is able to fulfil its deep and all-encompassing requirement.

The first commandment to have this extended application placed on it (that is, from actions to thoughts and words as well), is the sixth: "You shall not murder" (Exodus 20:13; Deuteronomy 5:17; Matthew 5:21–26). Here Jesus says that outward conformity to the commandment is of no value if a person bears anger, malice or contempt towards a fellow human being. Anyone who is angry with his or her brother will be subject to judgement. If a Jew is answerable to the Sanhedrin for cursing a fellow Israelite with the word "*Raca*",[43] then how much more liable will he be to eternal punishment for calling a brother a fool! Because of the seriousness of this judgement, it is essential to be reconciled with those with whom we are at enmity, otherwise our anger and hostility could be held against us eternally. For this reason, Jesus goes on to give two ways in which reconciliation might occur.

The first vignette Jesus offers is of a brother ("*adelphos*", meaning a fellow disciple and therefore a member of the church community) offering a gift in the temple, probably a sacrificial animal. This vivid vignette perhaps envisages someone from Galilee travelling all the way to Jerusalem to make this offering, before remembering that he is out of sorts with a fellow disciple. Recalling this, he journeys all the way back to Galilee to put his relationship straight before returning to make his offering in Jerusalem.

Of course, at one level it is a highly unlikely story, much like a camel going through the eye of a needle, but the very unlikelihood makes the point that, whatever the cost or inconvenience, relationships must be put right, and that there is no point carrying on with the normal life of discipleship and worship if in the background (or, indeed, in the foreground) there is a broken relationship in need of repair.

The second vignette painted by Jesus is of two people going to court—it is worth noticing in passing his manner of teaching in vivid and memorable examples to illustrate what can be done to avoid a breakdown in relationships. A dispute lies unresolved, possibly over the repayment of a debt. The person who is defrauded seeks to take the other to court. Jesus counsels that it is far better to settle out of court, since the accused might be thrown into prison until the last penny has been paid. Here Jesus implies that wherever possible, disputes should be settled out of court, dues paid and, if possible, relationships restored. To persist in the dispute and be taken to court is to risk losing everything, including our freedom. It is thus far better to be reconciled and to pay whatever is owing, thus settling the dispute, than to persist in a quarrel that is going nowhere except the courts. The lessons of this illustration are to settle disputes quickly, settle them out of court, and not get into a position where the courts will determine the outcome (see also Paul's similar teaching in 1 Corinthians 6:1–11).

If, in the previous section of teaching, Jesus has extended the sixth commandment to areas of speech and emotion, as well as to the obligation to be reconciled, the next section applies to the seventh commandment (5:27–30). Once again, the teaching begins with a restatement of the original: "You have heard that it was said, 'Do not commit adultery'" (Exodus 20:14; Deuteronomy 5:18). Jesus again extends the remit beyond simply our actions, to our thoughts as well. What exactly he means by "looking at a woman lustfully" needs further elucidation. Commentators believe this may refer to looking at a married woman in particular, but it could very well apply to any woman.[44] Looking lustfully presumably means wanting or planning to have sex with a woman. If either the woman (who is looked at) or the man (who is looking) is married, then such lustful looking is clearly a contravention of the seventh commandment.

By contrast, however, an unmarried person is normally planning and looking forward to having sex with their future spouse, as intimated in the Song of Songs. So is sexual desire the same as looking lustfully? Looking with desire upon one's affianced is clearly celebrated in the Song of Songs, in which case it is *how* a person looks with desire, rather than desire itself, that breaks the commandment (although many of the Early Church Fathers thought differently). The healthiness of the desire depends on the status of the couple concerned. Since faithfulness is a gold standard of sexual relationships in the Bible, wanting or planning sexual contact outside of this violates those relationships. The violation may be committed not only in deed, but also in intention or thought, according to Jesus.

The issue of desire in relation to sex has been variously treated in church history. The Church Fathers generally believed that all sex, even in marriage, was tainted by concupiscence—that is, lust—and that the only way out of such desire was virginity.[45] More recently, desire has been considered part of a healthy relationship, although to be expressed only between two partners in marriage. Such desire within marriage is legitimate, but wanting or planning to have sex outside marriage contravenes Jesus' teaching. His naming of immorality in this way is radical, and his treatment of it more radical still. He calls for cutting off the offending eye or hand rather than being led by them into "hell", or eternal loss. Some Early Church Fathers or ascetics took this suggestion literally: Origen is reputed to have castrated himself.

The rigorous nature of Jesus' teaching on sexual conduct leaves us with a considerable challenge. It is up to us individually to police the distinction between admiration of beauty and sexual indulgence; to distinguish between art (a female or male nude, such as Michelangelo's David or the Rokeby Venus by Velázquez) and pornography; to have good relationships with women and men, but to remain faithful to our partners; and to celebrate the gift of sex in the right place, but to keep it there. Jesus acknowledges here that unfaithfulness begins in the mind, and it is here that the battle for purity and faithfulness is fought and won, or lost. He makes us face up to our thinking long before our thoughts become actions. It is not surprising that Jesus' teaching then moves to the subject of divorce.

Divorce can be described as a subsection of the teaching on the sixth commandment. If Jesus extends its meaning to include our thoughts as well as our actions, he is no less demanding when it comes to divorce. Divorce, or granting a bill of divorce, is discussed in Deuteronomy 24:1–4 in terms of a man issuing a bill of divorce for a wife who has become displeasing to him, or because of "something indecent about her" (Deuteronomy 24:1). This phrase—"something indecent about her"—was variously interpreted by the rabbis in Jesus' day and, as one might imagine, much hung on it. The Hebrew phrase *"erwat-dabar"*, meaning something indecent in the woman, is at the root of the debate. The two schools of rabbinical thought are represented by Shammai (more conservative and strict) and Hillel (more liberal). Shammai believed that grounds for divorce could only be unchastity, whereas Hillel taught that it could be anything that is displeasing to the husband in his wife, since in the illustration in Deuteronomy 24, the second husband (who divorces the same woman) can do so purely on the grounds of disliking her. Jesus now interposes his teaching into this debate.

Whereas in Mark and Luke, Jesus gives no legitimate reason at all for divorce (Mark 10:1–12; Luke 16:18), in Matthew, Jesus teaches that there is one legitimate ground for divorce and that is the adultery of the wife (5:31–32; see also 19:1–12, especially v. 9). Because in Judaism a woman could not initiate divorce proceedings, a husband's adultery presumably could not, in practice, be grounds for divorce at the time, although we might expect the same failure to constitute a legitimate end of the marriage from the wife's side too. Jesus teaches that a marriage can be ended for "marital unfaithfulness", or literally *"logou porneia"*, a matter of fornication, the Greek equivalent of the phrase in Deuteronomy meaning "something indecent about her". Although neither the Church Fathers nor Roman Catholic teaching permitted the right to remarry after a divorce, the Jewish practice was that a divorce carried within it the implicit right to remarry. Thus someone who had divorced on these grounds was entitled to remarry, whereas anyone divorcing for any other reason (as permitted by Hillel) would be making both himself and his new wife guilty of adultery.

In his teaching Jesus upholds the provision that marriage is for life (Genesis 2:24), but gives this exception for divorce. The fact that "bills of divorce" (or, as we would say, "*decrees nisi*") are the occasion of divorces in the courts for various reasons is because of human hardness of heart. It is not God's plan for marriage from the beginning. In Jesus' own day his teaching was clearly rigorous, as the disciples themselves observe: "If this is the situation between a husband and wife, it is better not to marry" (Matthew 19:10). As with the other commandments he applies during the Sermon on the Mount, the standard Jesus upholds is more rather than less demanding.

Having applied the laws on murder and theft to our thoughts and expressions, Jesus moves on to consider the use of words, and in particular, oaths (5:33–37). His general position is that all oaths are superfluous, since a disciple is to speak truthfully on all matters, in which case no oath is needed. The general situation in Jesus' day was that people embellished their speech with a host of oaths. Oaths normally invoked God as the guarantor of the person's words, but a plethora of oaths then developed, tied to a kind of hierarchy of truth, depending on the attribution of the oath. Social swearing grew up, with people swearing by heaven or earth, or by Jerusalem or the altar in the temple, or by the hairs of their heads. Yet all these oaths are out of order since they either invoke God indirectly—the earth is God's footstool, the heavens are his throne, and Jerusalem is "the city of the great King"—or they invoke their own heads, including their hair, over which they have no control.

The underlying point about all these oaths is that we should not call on powers outside our control as witness in support of our words. It is like a child invoking a grandfather, much respected but long deceased, who can give no corroboration of the child's saying. In other words, oaths press-gang into service support that has simply not been given. It is therefore presumptuous and arrogant to use them. No, it is much better for the disciple to be known for her honesty, with no need for any oath. Her word is her bond. "Let your word be 'Yes, Yes' or 'No, No'; anything more than this comes from the evil one" (5:37, NRSV).

The final section of this teaching extending the impact of the law has to do with love and retribution (5:33–48). The effect of these two pieces of complementary teaching is to change radically the disciple's treatment of his or her opponents. Once again Jesus begins with the teaching of the Torah, which includes the law of reciprocal punishment, namely an eye

for an eye and a tooth for a tooth" (5:38, NRSV). This quotation is found
three times in the Greek version of the Old Testament, the Septuagint
(Exodus 21:24; Leviticus 24:20; Deuteronomy 19:21), and in each case
there is a longer list of equivalents. Exodus 21:23–25, for example, reads,
"If there is serious injury, you are to take life for life, eye for eye, tooth
for tooth, hand for hand, foot for foot, burn for burn, wound for wound,
bruise for bruise."

Jesus is therefore summarizing this legal principle of equivalent
punishment. But now he introduces something completely unlike what
has gone before: *a disciple is not even to resist an evil person* (5:39). Jesus
uses four quick-fire illustrations, memorable for their pithiness and
novelty, to show what he means by non-retaliation. The first illustration
is turning the other cheek—that is, if a person strikes your left cheek,
offer your right cheek to be struck as well by your assailant: do not resist.
Such a blow on the right cheek is deemed especially insulting, but the
disciple, like his master, is to offer no resistance (Isaiah 50:6). "In a culture
which took honour and shame far more seriously than ours, this was a
paradoxical and humiliating demand."[46]

The second illustration of non-retaliation is to offer your cloak as well
as your shirt to a legal adversary (5:40). The shirt, *"chiton"*, is the most
basic garment worn next to the skin and can be claimed by an adversary
as surety for a debt. But Jesus says that if someone claims it, you should
give him your much more valuable cloak, *"himation"*, which can double
as a sleeping bag. So valuable is the cloak in the Old Testament that if
it is taken as surety for paying a debt, it has to be returned by sunset, as
it is frequently a person's only night-time covering (Exodus 22:26–27;
Deuteronomy 24:12–13). Yet Jesus says, give it away to the person who
has wronged you! The point seems to be that it is better to be wronged
and defrauded than to initiate a lawsuit.

The third illustration has, like the first, passed into common language:
this one as "going the second mile" (5:41). During the Roman occupation
of Palestine in the first century, a Roman soldier could legally force a local
passer-by to carry his luggage or equipment for one mile. Jesus says a Jew
thus imposed upon should carry the burden not just *one* mile, but two.
Such an abject renunciation of personal rights—and for an occupying
Gentile force—is both unthinkable and incomprehensible. Yet Jesus

suggests it! Human pride, patriotic pride and ethnic pride—all come second to serving an enemy. This is shocking in its demand.

The last illustration is perhaps less shocking, but equally extravagant (5:42). To give to every beggar or loan-seeker might be thought to encourage dependency or gross irresponsibility. It is one thing to give a few coins to a beggar in the street, but it may be quite a different thing to give hundreds of pounds in unsecured loans. Yet Jesus appears to say we should err on the side of risky generosity rather than cautious circumspection. If money is being repeatedly given or loaned over time, it might be useful to discover the reason for the need and the best way of dealing with it. In any event, it seems we are not at liberty simply to walk away from the request without helping in the best way we can.

The general principle arising from these illustrations appears to be that in the kingdom, self-interest comes second to extraordinary sacrificial service. There are few requests by Jesus to judge or discriminate against others. Instead, there is an overriding call to offer no personal resistance, to give extravagantly, to serve sacrificially, and to be vulnerable in the process. It is hardly worldly-wise or "sensible", but it is in keeping with the topsy-turvy kingdom we are called to demonstrate.

Jesus goes one step further in defining love in a way that was, and remains, revolutionary. Simply put, the command here is to "love your enemies and pray for those who persecute you" (5:44).The justification for such a response to hostility or worse is seen in the example of the disciples' heavenly Father: "He causes his sun to rise on the evil and the good, and sends rain on the righteous and the unrighteous" (5:45). In other words, he does not discriminate between those with whom he shares his blessings of rain or sunshine. Both good and evil enjoy his blessings.

Likewise, a disciple is to show love towards and pray for those who persecute him. Imprisoned and suffering Christians have done this. The Romanian pastor Richard Wurmbrand told how, though beaten with truncheons by his prison guards in the 1950s, he responded with love. In the end, the love of God he demonstrated was more persuasive than the captors' rods. His captors were changed more by love than those persecuted Christians were changed by violence.[47] If we restrict ourselves to loving only those who love us, and not those who despise us or abuse us, then we are no better than pagans. Disciples are to become like their heavenly Father, to be perfect as he is. In the end, the disciple is not following rules, but in his or her thinking, speaking and acting is becoming like God himself. This is only possible through his grace working in us; anything less is to fall short of the true calling of God.

In this way Jesus fulfils the law, doing so supremely in his own Passion and sufferings: turning his other cheek, going more than the extra mile, carrying not luggage but the cross, praying for his enemies and those who crucify him, speaking plainly of his mission. He fulfils the law in every way. He calls us, his disciples, to do the same in a new way and prompted by a new golden rule: "In everything, do to others what you would have them do to you, for this sums up [fulfils] the law and the Prophets" (7:12).

To be perfect is not open to us. It is a calling we can embrace but cannot perfectly fulfil (5:48). Nor can we serve or follow by the old written code. The law, through Christ, has been extended to our thoughts, motives and words, so even to begin to fulfil this most taxing demand we need the power of the Spirit and the forgiveness of the cross (Romans 8:1–4). This is part of the calling of a disciple and it points to the kingdom Christ promises.

CHAPTER 5

The Presence of the Future—
The Kingdom of God

Matthew 8—9

Immediately following his extensive teachings on discipleship, grouped together as the Sermon on the Mount, the authority of Jesus is further displayed, not primarily as a teacher, but as the inaugurator of the kingdom he has come to bring and to demonstrate. He has come to bring a *taste* of the kingdom for which he encouraged his disciples to pray (6:10). What follows in Matthew 8—9 is a sequence of quick-fire events—all miracles—that make clear both his authority and the nature of the kingdom.

Healing plays a dominant role in Jesus' ministry. In the space of two chapters, he heals a leper, heals the centurion's servant from a distance, heals a crowd of sick people who gather at the house of Simon Peter (as well as healing Simon's mother-in-law), heals two demon-possessed men and a paralytic, raises to life a dead girl, heals a woman with a haemorrhage, and finally heals two blind men and one dumb man. It's an impressive range of healings covering a wide spectrum of illnesses, including demon possession, and even raising the dead. Collectively, these healings show "the presence of the future": of a kingdom in which there is no more pain, disease, death or exclusion. Individually, as we shall see, each of these healings pushes back the boundaries of human suffering with the invasion of a kingdom of power and restoration.

The leper

On the way down the mountainside, a leper finds Jesus (8:1–4). Leprosy is still a common disease today: it destroys nerve endings leading to visible and shocking damage to limbs and extremities—hands, feet and face. This leper approaches Jesus with considerable faith and understanding; we are told he kneels before or worships him.[48] The man calls Jesus "Lord" or "*kyrie*"; he has no doubt that Jesus can heal him. Jesus has the power, but the leper asks if Jesus has the will. In asking this, the unnamed leper wants to know if Jesus' compassion extends to the likes of him, since—as we are aware—people with contagious skin diseases were ostracized and excluded from Jewish society. Jesus leaves him in no doubt, saying yes, he is willing, and he stretches out his hand to touch him (8:3). By these actions of reaching out and touching, Jesus shows his compassion to all with this disease. Like those doctors and celebrities who touched people with HIV/AIDS in the 1980s, he demonstrates inclusion, but more than that, he has the power to cleanse and cure the leper, removing the cause of his ostracism. Three times Matthew uses the word "*katharistheti*" (8:2–3) meaning "cleansing", the Greek root of our noun "catharsis". The healing of Jesus is therefore to cleanse not only the physical, but also the psychological damage this man has endured. After all, the law prescribes that a person with such a disease is to have his hair uncut, his clothes torn, his face covered, and is to cry out wherever he goes, "Unclean, unclean!" He must live alone and outside any village or town. Such exclusion can only have worsened his mental state. So to bring this healing home to the man, as well as to the community, he is required by the law to go and show himself to the priest (see Leviticus 13:45–46; 14:1–32). By presenting himself to the priest, the healing can be confirmed, and he can be welcomed back into the community.

In healing the man with leprosy, Jesus demonstrates his power and willingness to heal, and shows that the kingdom includes those who by virtue of sickness are not only ill, but have been excluded from the community. No longer will the victim of this disease cry, "Unclean, unclean!" but instead will be incorporated into a new community where he will be accepted.

The second incident Matthew records in chapter 8 is Jesus' meeting with the centurion in Capernaum, and the healing at a distance of the centurion's servant (8:5–13). Centurions were the staff sergeants of the Roman army, brought into existence by the Marian Reforms of the army in 107 BC. They commanded about eighty men apiece, the vital unit in the composition of the army, part of the larger components of cohorts, and then legions. There were no Roman legions based in Palestine; they were based in Antioch, the capital of the Eastern Empire before the founding of Constantinople nearly three hundred years later. There was a Governor of Judea, and both he and Herod Antipas had troops available to them. Almost invariably in the Gospels and Acts, centurions receive a good press. Of this centurion, Jesus famously says, "I have not found anyone in Israel with such great faith" (8:10). The centurion supervising the crucifixion of Christ confesses, "Surely this man was the Son of God!" (Mark 15:39; see also Matthew 27:54), and of course, it was Cornelius, a centurion in Roman Caesarea, who was the first Gentile to be admitted into the kingdom of God, together with his household and friends, by virtue of the gift of the Spirit (Acts 10:44). Here in Matthew, the centurion demonstrates his unusual faith by saying that there is no need for Jesus to come to his house to heal his servant—"Just say the word, and my servant will be healed" (8:8b). The centurion does not feel it is fitting for Jesus to come to his house, since he is a Gentile and Jesus is a Jew. Recognizing the authority of Jesus as equivalent to his own, by which a command is immediately and obediently fulfilled, the centurion has no problem with Jesus healing his servant using a word of command from a distance. A military man recognizes authority when he sees it. It is this faith and confidence that astonishes Jesus: the centurion has a practical, working faith in the ability of Jesus to perform whatever he wishes to do.

Demonstrating his desire to show the Jews that the salvation offered by Jesus is for all people everywhere, Matthew does not leave this miracle here. He draws a further point from the faith of the centurion about the dynamic that is at work. This kingdom is for all people who believe in the king. Matthew records Jesus' revolutionary saying that the messianic banquet-to-come will no longer be a Jewish affair with no Gentiles present, but that people will come "from the east and the west" (8:11), that is, from throughout the world, and will take up places in this banquet of the kingdom. Others who think they have a permanent right to be there, and who are "members of the club", will find themselves excluded, indeed, thrown into outer darkness (8:12). Matthew, typically, does not let the centurion's faith rest on its own merits, but goes on to make the case that he is indicative of a new movement in which the Gentiles will overtake the Jewish people in their admittance to the kingdom.

The next example of healing in these two chapters is that of two demon-possessed men in the region of the Gadarenes (8:28–34). Once again this healing illustrates the authority of Jesus, previously emphasized in this chapter in the miracle of the stilling of the storm (8:23–27). Later we will especially consider wider aspects of this authority of Jesus, which is another great theme of Matthew's Gospel (see 28:18–20). Here we see the deliverance of the two demon-possessed men as a further sign of the breaking in of the kingdom Jesus has come to inaugurate. The story of this healing varies from its Markan and Lukan equivalents (Mark 5:1–20; Luke 8:26–39). In both these accounts, which occur at a similar moment after Jesus crosses the lake and stills the storm, there is a single demoniac, and both Mark and Luke tell of his deliverance in much greater detail and far more vividly. Matthew, who we believe had Mark's account available to him, decides to tell the story with less detail, presumably on the grounds of having another source (oral or written) which tells of two Gadarene demoniacs. R. T. France comments on this account, and a similar instance of a single blind man "becoming" two blind men in Matthew 20:29–34, saying, "I do not know of any really satisfactory explanation of Matthew's tendency to see double."[49]

Although there may be no satisfactory way of explaining why Matthew reports the healing of two demoniacs in the way he does, there is no doubting the main point: the authority of Jesus over all the works of darkness, and evil spirits in particular. Jesus crosses to the Decapolis: ten cities on the eastern side of Galilee populated by a mixture of Jews and Gentiles, hence the presence of pigs there. It is one of the excursions made by Jesus out of strictly Jewish territory into the hinterland of Israel; another one is to the vicinity of Tyre (15:21–28). In both areas he heals people, although recognizing that he is beyond the territory of Israel which is his principal place of ministry. The area where the demon-possessed are healed is variously described by the Gospel writers as being in the vicinity of Gadara or Gerasa, both towns in the Decapolis.[50]

In Matthew's very truncated version of the healing, the evil spirits immediately recognize Jesus, as they do elsewhere in the Gospels (see Mark 1:24, for example). They fear that they will be tortured and plead to be allowed into the herd of pigs. There is no question of doing other than the command of Jesus. They do indeed go into the herd of pigs; the animals then rush down the hillside into the lake and perish. There is none of the dialogue between Jesus and the demoniac that we find in Mark and Luke, nor a description of his state of being before and after the healing, so the account in Matthew loses much of its compelling, personal power. The loss of the pigs and the hit to the local economy is much more to the fore in Matthew than the transformation of the demoniacs themselves (8:34). The question arises as to why Matthew tells the story the way he does. Why is there none of the touching detail (present in Mark and Luke) of the rehabilitation of the man from his sub-human life to his quiet faith in Jesus, and his willingness to become one of his disciples and evangelists? These are surely the questions most of us would want to ask.

The answer is probably that Matthew has a single overall purpose in describing this miracle, and that is to emphasize the authority and power of Jesus. Thus it is not a story about how Jesus delivers the men, or one about the effects of mission—of how Jesus can make us fully human and rescue us from the damaging power of the devil—but rather, for Matthew, this exorcism has the single purpose of demonstrating Jesus' power. It is not a power welcomed by the people of the Decapolis; nor was it a power always welcomed by his opponents in Israel (9:34). This reminds us that, for all its restorative power, not everyone welcomes the kingdom of heaven.

After Jesus has healed the Gadarene demoniacs, he returns to Capernaum, the centre of his Galilean ministry. As soon as he steps out of the boat, he is met by a group of men who bring him a paralysed man lying on a mat (9:1–8). They come with faith (9:2), which will be rewarded by the healing of their friend. Unusually, Jesus prefaces his healing with a statement combining both encouragement and mention of sin. First he says, "Take heart, son," or more literally, "Be of good cheer, child."

Calling the paralysed man "child" underscores the fact that he is both a child of Abraham and/or a child of God, but it also has the effect of being a reassuring form of address, rather like saying, "It's all right, lad!" However, this endearing informality is coupled with the more realistic and forbidding statement, "Your sins are forgiven."

Jesus discerns a link between this man's paralysis and the need for forgiveness. However, it is this claim to forgive sins that provokes the local religious leaders or teachers of the law to object that Jesus is blaspheming, since only God has the right to forgive sins. Observing their reaction from their body language, Jesus poses them a challenge. He makes the healing of the paralysed man a confirmation of his authority to forgive sins. Both forgiving sins and healing someone with paralysis require divine authority, and Jesus confirms the former claim—to forgive sins—by the latter action—healing the man who was paralysed.

In the process of confirming his authority to forgive sins, he refers to himself as the Son of Man: a favourite title of Jesus, drawn from the visions of Daniel (Daniel 7:13–14). In his vision, Daniel sees a figure who shares absolute authority with the Father Almighty—termed the "Most High" (7:18,22) or the "Ancient of Days" (7:13,22)—who is described as "one like a son of man". His authority is over all peoples and nations of every language, and his task is to establish an everlasting dominion or kingdom that will never be destroyed (7:14). Thus the sceptical body language of a few religious leaders in Galilee brings about a response that is truly awesome in its perspective. Jesus makes the indirect claim that he is none other than the Son of Man, who is charged with establishing this eternal kingdom. Healing this paralysed man by way of forgiving his sins is a further step in demonstrating this kingdom and bringing the assured future into the present.

Having made the claim to forgive sins, and linking this to the cure of the paralysed man, Jesus commands him to get up off his bed and go home. The anonymous man does so, amazing the crowds who marvel and are fearful at such authority displayed by a human being. The underlying question is framed by the crowd's reaction: is Jesus *just* a human being?

The next healing miracle in this sequence—and we shall return shortly to the other events of the two chapters which Matthew weaves in with the miracles—is a miracle of raising the dead. This miraculous resurrection envelops, in the text, the separate healing of a woman with a haemorrhage (9:18–26). In each of the Synoptic Gospels these two miracles are interwoven, and each story has the implicit theme of Jesus' attitude to ritual purity, since both a dead body and the issue of blood make anyone who has contact with them ritually unclean. Nevertheless, Jesus has contact with both, and each is restored to life in different ways: the young girl literally, and the older woman by having her social restrictions removed. Giving life is more important than ritual purity; fulfilling the law is best done through mercy and not sacrifice, keeping its spirit and not just its letter, as Jesus will tell the Pharisees later (23:23).

While Jesus is teaching about fasting (9:14–17), he is interrupted by an urgent request from a ruler of the local synagogue (named as Jairus by Mark and Luke), who kneels before Jesus, telling him that his daughter has just died (9:18). In Mark and Luke's Gospels, the father is told of the death of his daughter en route to his house (Mark 5:35; Luke 8:49), but in Matthew's much more terse and low-key account of these two stories, Jesus is told of the death of the daughter at the outset. It might be legitimate to ask why his account of the healing of the Gadarene demoniac(s) and of these two healings is so much terser than Mark's and Luke's. Once again, it could be that Matthew has less interest in conveying the human story of the main figures in the account, and that his simple aim is to describe the authority of Jesus.

Matthew tells the story of the woman with the issue of blood much more succinctly. In Mark and Luke her touching of Jesus is secret, and in Mark her own internal conversation is more pronounced (Mark 5:28). Both Luke and Mark portray her as being at her wits' end, having spent all her savings on doctors who are unable to cure her (Mark 5:26; Luke 8:43, with variant reading). In each of the Synoptic Gospels, Jesus greets the woman warmly once she is known and has emerged from the crowd. Once again, Mark and Luke describe fully the process of bringing the woman into the open to admit her healing (Mark 5:30–34; Luke 8:45–48), and likewise Jesus' own perception of power having gone out from him. In Matthew, neither of these explanations occurs. On the one hand, we could say that Matthew is not a consummate storyteller in his use of the material available to him or, on the other, we could say that his purpose in these chapters is to establish both the coming of the kingdom and the authority of Jesus in a cascade of miracles, and this is his overriding purpose rather than embellishing them with human detail.

When Jesus arrives at the house of the synagogue ruler, whose daughter has died, a further issue is added to the narrative with Jesus saying outright that the girl is not dead, only sleeping (9:24; Mark 5:39; Luke 8:52). Sleep appears to be a metaphor for death; Jesus may have called this sleep knowing he will soon raise her to life again, or it may be a general way of describing death as being like sleep. The apostle Paul calls the Christian dead "those who have fallen asleep in him" (1 Thessalonians 4:14). In any event, Jesus regards the girl's death as being like sleep. Death, like sleep, does not have an eternal grip, but will be ended by the power of resurrection and new life. Not only that, but Jesus has authority over death's grip as over sickness, and can wake from death those whom he chooses.

In the Gospels we have three accounts of people being brought back to life: the son of the widow of Nain (Luke 7:11–17), Lazarus (John 11:1–44), and this raising of Jairus' daughter. Now Jesus proves that the girl may be wakened from this "sleep" since he has authority over death. Taking the three inner-circle disciples into the room, and putting the professional mourners outside, Jesus restores the girl to life, holding her hand. Once again, the Markan story is much fuller—here Jesus addresses the girl in Aramaic, saying "*Talitha koum!*", which means, "Little girl, I say to you, get up!" (Mark 5:41). Luke, the doctor, tells us at this point that her spirit returns to her body (Luke 8:55), underscoring the notion that death is marked by a separation of body from spirit. Once again, the crowd is astonished at this great reversal.

The final healings in Matthew's whistle-stop tour of the ministry of Jesus in Galilee are of two blind men and one dumb man (9:27–34). It is as if, in the space of these two chapters, Matthew wants to tell us of the sheer scope of Jesus' healing power, which is also a demonstration of his just, gentle and powerful rule or kingdom. The two blind men follow Jesus, addressing him by his Messianic title, "Son of David", just as blind Bartimaeus does in Mark's Gospel (Mark 10:47). However, it is only when they are inside a building that Jesus questions them as to whether they have faith that he can heal them (9:28). They reply that they do, and Jesus restores their sight as he touches their eyes. He then sternly warns them not to tell anyone, but in their great joy they broadcast the news of their healing everywhere they go.

Leaving the house, Jesus is confronted by a demon-possessed man who is dumb and is brought by friends. Knowing the cause of his inability to speak, Jesus drives out the demon, and the man's speech is restored. The crowd is full of praise, but the opponents of Jesus say he can drive out evil spirits because he is himself the prince of demons. It is an argument they will develop further later (12:22–29), but Jesus blows this argument and slur out of the water. If he were casting out demons as their prince, it would be like a house divided against itself that would not stand (12:26). Since he drives out demons by the Holy Spirit, the kingdom of God has come upon them. (This is one of the few instances where Matthew uses the term "kingdom of God" rather than the more Jewish "kingdom of heaven", which avoids the naming of the Almighty.)

For Matthew, these healing miracles are all part of showing the authority of Jesus over sickness, death and the devil; of making known and establishing the kingdom (9:35; 12:28), and in so doing fulfilling the words of the prophet Isaiah, who said, "He took up our infirmities and carried our diseases" (8:17, quoting Isaiah 53:4). Yet even when Jesus has healed many, as he does outside the house of Peter, there are many more whom he sees as "harassed and helpless", and upon whom he has compassion (9:36). To meet their needs, and those of wider humanity, he must now commission followers to do what he has done: to teach in the synagogues, preach the good news, and heal every disease and sickness. The harvest is plentiful but the workers are few; he must therefore send out workers or disciples to take on these tasks in his name (see 9:35–38 and the following chapter).

CHAPTER 6

The Authority of Jesus

*Matthew 8:23–27; 14:22–36; 14:13–21 and
15:29–39; 11:25–30; 12:15–21*

*(If you are studying in a group, these passages could be read
by different people in the above order, before answering
the questions found in the back of the book.)*

There is no doubt that one of the great themes of Matthew's Gospel is the
authority of Jesus. This theme culminates in Jesus' famous saying at the
end of the Gospel, "All authority in heaven and on earth has been given
to me" (28:18). This authority has already been amply shown throughout
the Gospel and is especially evident in Jesus' power over creation around
Galilee, the healing miracles we have witnessed, and the demands he
places on his disciples. As we shall see, this authority is also wrapped in
humility, as prophesied by Isaiah.

The authority of Jesus over creation is particularly clearly demonstrated
in events around Galilee. The climate of that region gives Jesus ample
opportunity to show his power over the weather, especially the wind and
the lake. The first incident is when Jesus calms a violent storm (8:23–27).
Lake Galilee, or the Sea of Tiberias (named after the Roman Emperor
during whose reign Jesus' ministry took place), is situated well below sea
level in the steep-sided Rift Valley. This rift begins in the Beqaa Valley
in present-day Lebanon, and runs along the Jordan Valley through the
Dead Sea, all the way to Mozambique in Africa, some 6,000 kilometres
in length. The Sea of Galilee is subject to sudden, violent squalls, and
the resulting turbulence is dangerous to shallow fishing boats. Although

generally quiet and calm, the Sea of Galilee can change dramatically and dangerously.

One such occasion is described by Matthew, when Jesus embarks in a boat with the disciples and a furious storm is suddenly whipped up by the wind, with the waves breaking over the sides (8:24). Amazingly, Jesus—who has fallen asleep—continues to sleep until woken by his disciples who fear for their lives. But he says to them, "You of little faith, why are you so afraid?" He rebukes the wind and the waves, whereupon the weather becomes calm. No wonder the disciples are in awe of this demonstration of Jesus' authority over the natural order, wondering, "What kind of man is this? Even the winds and the waves obey him!" (8:27).

I heard recently of a not-dissimilar incident. On the north coast of Devon, a group got into difficulties on a cliff overhanging the sea. A member of the group lost his footing in a high wind, and fell. He found himself on a ledge high above the sea, hanging on for dear life to the scrubby bushes growing there. One of the group rang for the emergency rescue services, and a helicopter came, but it was so windy the winchman could not be safely lowered to within striking distance of the ledge. Remembering the example of Jesus, the group addressed the wind, praying for it to cease, and amazingly the wind dropped. The winchman was then lowered to the ledge, and the man saved from his predicament.

Another example of Jesus showing his authority and power over the natural order comes a little later in the Gospel. Once again it happens on the Sea of Galilee. Jesus has dismissed the crowds after feeding the five thousand, and has gone up into the hills to pray, sending the disciples on ahead by boat to cross to the other side of the lake (14:22–23). The disciples once again find themselves rowing against a strong wind and making painful progress. During the fourth watch of the night, which is a Roman term for the period between 3 a.m. and 6 a.m., Jesus comes to the disciples, walking on the water. Presumably they have been rowing for the best part of nine hours, and are well out into the lake and quite possibly nearing the other side. The lake is about twenty-one kilometres long and thirteen kilometres wide. Against the wind it has been a long and arduous row. At this point Jesus draws level with them, walking on the water. At first they think he is a ghost, but Jesus reassures them. Peter asks to walk to him on the water, but having taken just a few steps, is overwhelmed by the wind and the enormity of what he is attempting, and begins to sink. Crying out to Jesus, he is saved from going under. It is a familiar story, which once again exemplifies the power Jesus has over creation. To walk on water is to suspend the normal laws of physics, but such laws bend to the will of the one in whom all laws of the physical universe adhere or are held together (Colossians 1:17; John 1:3). Alongside the miracle of the event itself, demonstrating Jesus' authority over the elements, there are plenty of encouragements to faith: to get out of the boat; to keep our eyes fixed on Jesus rather than on the forces that intimidate, and not to doubt (14:29–32). The response of the disciples to this miracle is a spontaneous, "Truly you are the Son of God" (14:33). What appears here to be a reflexive confession of the authority of Jesus becomes a more formal and considered confession of Jesus as *the Christ* two chapters later, in the question Jesus poses in Caesarea Philippi.

These two wonders performed by Jesus on Lake Galilee are complemented by the most famous of all his miracles, the feeding of the multitude. This miracle appears in all the Gospels, but Matthew and Mark include both the feeding of the five *and* the four thousand (Matthew 14:13–21 and 15:29–39; Mark 6:30–44 and 8:1–10; Luke 9:10–17; John 6:1–13). Once again it is a miracle with a clear teaching purpose. Some commentators, such as the German Liberal Protestant theologian David Friedrich Strauss (1808–1874), have denied the validity of the miracle, claiming that the disciples fed the crowd from a cave filled with hidden supplies! Yet the Gospel writers themselves have no doubt about the historicity of the miracle, and for Matthew and Mark it happens on two occasions. The miracle points once again to the authority of Jesus over creation, multiplying a limited supply of food to feed five thousand men, women and children. Such provision from five barley loaves and two fish is beyond scientific comprehension. If a miracle is the suspension of normal physical laws through the intervention of divine power, then the feeding of thousands from a few rolls and a bit of fish is a clear demonstration of this. Science cannot readily explain the process, but faith can believe.

The feeding of the five thousand (14:13–21) comes at the end of a full day's teaching and healing. Earlier that day, Jesus has sought solitude to consider the news of the gratuitous execution of his cousin, John the Baptist, carried out to satisfy the revenge of Herodias (14:1–12). He has taken a boat to a solitary place to think and pray, and quite possibly to consider what this news means for him. As so often happens, his presence is sought by the crowd. We are told that he "had compassion on them and healed their sick" (14:14). This recalls what Matthew has written earlier: that "when [Jesus] saw the crowds, he had compassion on them, because they were harassed and helpless, like sheep without a shepherd" (9:36). At the end of the day the disciples become agitated about detaining the crowd, and suggest that Jesus should dismiss them, as there are no shops in the vicinity where they might buy food. Jesus challenges them to feed this vast crowd themselves, but after a quick inspection they find only a boy's packed lunch of five rolls and two fish, and what are those among so many? Making the crowd sit down in groups, the disciples act as waiters, distributing the bread and fish. The miracle appears to happen in their hands, with the food multiplied many times over. All are satisfied, and twelve basketfuls of leftovers are collected up at the end. In the parallel miracle with the four thousand (15:29–39), the numbers may be different but the principles are the same.

The feeding of the multitude is a multi-textured event. It recalls the provision of manna to the Israelites in the desert wanderings (Exodus 16). As with Moses, and now with Jesus, the people are fed. In recalling the gift of manna (literally meaning "What is it?"), the crowd—like the disciples—are asking a deeper question: "Who is this?" (8:27). John makes more of this than Matthew, recalling Jesus saying that he is the bread of life, giving life to the world (John 6:33,35). The miracle is also a test of the disciples—indeed, John makes this explicit (John 6:6). This provision will extend their faith, and it will demonstrate the classic lesson that a little goes a long way in the hands of Jesus. We must not be put off by the vulnerability or weakness of our offering, as long as it is placed in his hands. Finally, the occasion suggests the creation of a new community bound together by common nourishment. In that sense, the feeding of the five thousand anticipates another Eucharist (see 14:19, ". . . he gave thanks"—or blessed the Father—"and broke the loaves."), in which Jesus offers his body, symbolized by bread, as food for the world in a newly constituted fellowship based on a new covenant. The hillside meal at the end of a full day is thus a foretaste of a heavenly banquet to come.

If Jesus shows his authority by stilling the storm, walking on water and multiplying the loaves and fishes, he also shows it by establishing his authority over the Sabbath (12:1–13). The Sabbath is in the creation narrative of Genesis (God rested on the seventh day from all his work), and as such it is an institution that is part of the rhythm of life, which we ignore at our peril and at the cost of our wellbeing or flourishing. Besides their worship, there are three distinctive features that characterize the lives of the Jews. These are their food laws, circumcision and the observance of the Sabbath. All of these are spelt out in the Torah. The question, then, is not *whether* to observe the Sabbath, but *how* to do so. Two illustrations follow showing what this amounts to in practice: one is to do with refreshment, the other with healing.

Interestingly, these two back-to-back stories that deal with the issue of how to observe the Sabbath follow Jesus' own teaching about "rest" (11:28–30). To find "rest" means to find wholeness of being and ease of soul. Jesus encourages us to come to him and in that way to find rest for our souls. This is in contrast to the ways of the Pharisees, who take the call to rest on the Sabbath as a call to obey copious legislation surrounding Sabbath observance. The Pharisees became the leaders of the Jewish community from the second century BC. Their party existed "to promote and practice the most rigorous observance of the Torah, and the scribal elaborations of the law derived from the same ideological stable".[51] In their enforcement of rest on the Sabbath, they proscribed thirty-nine categories of activity classified as work. These activities included writing two letters, building or pulling down structures, carrying anything from one place to another, and travelling more than a Sabbath day's journey, which was construed as about half a mile.[52] Jesus now sets aside this approach to the Sabbath. He claims to have authority over the Sabbath as its Lord (12:8). He proclaims his sovereignty over the Sabbath as Creator, with the right to decide what is permissible. In essence, Jesus says it is permissible to do good on the Sabbath (12:12), and this is his underlying approach, unlike the scribal and pharisaic industry of Sabbath regulations. He demonstrates this in two ways.

The first way that Jesus and his disciples confront the regulatory approach to the Sabbath is by picking corn from the fields and eating it when they are hungry (12:1–8). The issue is not that they might be stealing, for there is provision in the law for the poor and hungry to glean from a field (Deuteronomy 23:25; Leviticus 23:22), but whether this gleaning is tantamount to reaping corn, which is prohibited on the Sabbath, and whether rubbing the grain out of the husks in their fingers is the same as threshing, another of the many forbidden Sabbath activities (Exodus 34:21)! Jesus responds to the accusation by the Pharisees that he and the disciples are Sabbath-breakers by citing two Old Testament precedents. The first is David eating the shewbread (or ceremonial bread of the Presence) in the tabernacle with the permission of Ahimelech the priest (1 Samuel 21:1–6), although it is only supposed to be eaten by the priests (Leviticus 24:9). The point here is not that David breaks the Sabbath, so much as that David, by virtue of his calling to be king, has the right to change the rules or customs. How much more, then, may the Son of David, who is Lord of the Sabbath, determine what is permissible on that day? Jesus is guided by the principle of the prophets—"I desire mercy, not sacrifice" (Hosea 6:6)—which heralds a fundamental distinction between Jesus and the religious leaders, to which we shall return.

The second illustration of Jesus' attitude to the Sabbath follows hard on the heels of the first. Jesus goes into the synagogue in Capernaum, where he is confronted by a man with a withered hand (12:9–14). Even before Jesus heals this man, the Pharisees get in their question: "Is it lawful to heal on the Sabbath?"(12:10). In Mark and Luke's telling of this story, we are only told that the Pharisees give silent opposition (Mark 3:1–6; Luke 6:6–11), to which Jesus responds. In Matthew's Gospel, Jesus responds to their spoken criticism. Although healing is not included in the thirty-nine forbidden acts on the Sabbath, it was not generally allowed. Healing was only to be given if there was fear of death or if a woman in labour required help. In response, Jesus draws a general principle based on common sense: people will rescue an animal in difficulties on the Sabbath if, for example, it has fallen down a well. Thus one ruling in the stricter Qumran community Jesus does *not* endorse decrees that "[n]o one may help an animal to give birth on the sabbath; and if it falls into a well or into a pit he may not lift it out on the sabbath."[53] This is an extreme ruling, however, and one which is against Jesus' basic attitude towards the Sabbath. He pronounces the Sabbath a day on which to do good; and, if common sense dictates that you will save an animal in difficulties on the Sabbath, how much more should you help a person, who is of much greater value than an animal! It is straightforward logic, based on the premise that the Sabbath is made for human beings and not human beings for the Sabbath (Mark 2:27). For us it begs the question, "How are we to find a day of rest each week, and what might such a day look like?"

Jesus then heals the man instantaneously with the minimum of work: simply with a word. The man's arm is completely restored, but the Pharisees—incensed by Jesus' unwillingness to toe their line, leave the place thinking how they might bring charges against him, or even kill him. Jesus, aware of their intentions, withdraws from there, but continues to heal the sick among those who follow him.

Before we return to these verses, there is one more way in which Jesus shows his authority: in the calling of the disciples and the demands he places on them. As with the other Synoptic Gospel writers, Matthew does not give a comprehensive list of the twelve apostles till later in his Gospel (see Mark 3:13–18; Luke 6:12–16). We noted the calling of Simon Peter, Andrew, James and John in Matthew 4:18–22. In chapter 9, Matthew tells of his own calling from the tax collector's booth (9:9–13). Yet there is no definitive list of the apostles in Matthew's Gospel until they are sent out by Jesus (10:2–4). In the previous verse, the vocation of the apostles is outlined as Jesus gives them authority to drive out evil spirits and to heal every disease.

The expectations laid by Jesus on the apostles are no less demanding in Matthew than in Mark or Luke. As with all disciples, they must put him first, before mother and father (8:22). Discipleship, they are told, may well bring division in the family (10:34–39). Losing your life in the service of Jesus will lead to finding it. Placing such demands on his disciples would be perverse *unless* Jesus had the right as the Son of God to do so. The fact that Jesus expects such discipleship and that it is reasonable, even though all-embracing, is further proof of his authority as the Messiah. No other prophet, teacher, Pharisee or religious leader could justify such a requirement from others.

The authority of Jesus is declared on every page of the Gospel: in his teaching, his lordship over creation, his many miracles of healing and in his right to call the apostles—and disciples in general—to such an unreserved devotion. It is an authority wrapped in compassion, however; a power cloaked in humility, and so, once again, Matthew describes how Jesus fulfils the prophecies of Isaiah (12:15–21). It is not surprising that Matthew, who is so familiar with the Old Testament, selects this part of the "servant songs" from Isaiah. The verses he chooses stress the gentleness of the Servant:

> He will not cry or lift up his voice, or make it heard in the street; a bruised reed he will not break, and a dimly burning wick he will not quench; he will faithfully bring forth justice.
>
> *Isaiah 42:2–3 (NRSV)*

The ministry of Jesus and the authority with which he exercises it are clothed in gentleness and humility. Indeed, only in the previous chapter Jesus famously says:

> "Come to me, all you that are weary and are carrying heavy burdens, and I will give you rest. Take my yoke upon you, and learn from me; for I am gentle and humble in heart, and you will find rest for your souls. For my yoke is easy, and my burden is light."
>
> *Matthew 11:28–30 (NRSV)*

Authority exercised in true gentleness and humility is subsequently to be a hallmark of all true Christian ministry. Arrogance, lording it over others, and superiority are not part of Christian leadership. "Not so with you," says Jesus. "Instead, whoever wants to become great among you must be your servant, and whoever wants to be first must be your slave" (20:24–28). Quite unlike the way authority was exercised in either the pagan or the Roman world, the exercise of authority or power within the kingdom is always to be a model of humility and gentleness. It is a new, radical Christian distinctive that Christ and Christianity bring to the world. Never before has humility been part of the function of power, but now it is! Nor has the call for such exercise of authority changed.

The distinguishing characteristic of Jesus' authority is that it not only achieves the purpose of his will, but it does so with the humility of a servant and the gentleness of a child—for "[a] bruised reed he will not break, and a smouldering wick he will not snuff out" (Matthew 12:20; Isaiah 42:3). With such authority, clothed in such humility, the growth of the kingdom is assured.

CHAPTER 7

Parables of the Kingdom

Matthew 13:1–58

The main teaching of Jesus' ministry is about the kingdom of God. It is teaching made known in both word and action (13:54). Jesus demonstrates the nature of this coming rule of God, or kingdom, by his miracles which display the presence of the future. He describes the kingdom's character in parables: its grace, its growth, and the crisis it will precipitate. Spoken originally in Aramaic and then translated into Greek, these parables recall a way of life typical of his day. They are a model form of communication and have the effect of hiding their truth or secrets from those who will not truly listen (see 13:11–17). They are not only windows into the mind of Christ and his teaching about the kingdom, but also vivid portrayals of a way of life familiar to his listeners, although often with a surprising twist.

Matthew clusters his parables mainly in two places. In Chapter 13 he brings together parables which are for the most part about the growth of the kingdom. Those included later in his Gospel (which we shall consider in the chapter on fulfilling the future) are about the coming crisis: the rejection of the Messiah and the judgement to come (21:28–46; 22:1–14; 25). Between these two groups, Matthew records some other parables describing the conduct of life in the church community, which we shall look at in Chapter 10. Here we concentrate on the parables about growth in the kingdom.

This cluster begins with the most well-known of Jesus' parables on growth, the Parable of the Sower—or, as some say, of the various soils. Another title could be given to reveal its more hidden yet fundamental meaning: the Parable of the Assured Harvest. The parable itself is told with little introduction by Jesus (13:1–9). Like Mark (4:10–12), Matthew then interposes both a question to Jesus from the disciples as to *why* he speaks in parables and Jesus' important answer (13:10–17), to which we shall return at the end of this chapter.

Jesus now explains the parable (13:18–23). The seed is the word, which alights on different soils. The first soil is akin to a hard path from which Satan easily snatches the word. This is like a person who does not receive the word deeply, but leaves it on the surface of their life, vulnerable to it being snatched away. The second soil is rocky ground where the seed cannot take root and therefore does not flourish. The third soil is full of weeds, representing the cares of this life and the deceitfulness of riches, which strangle and suffocate the seed .The final soil is good, and it bears fruit in different quantities: thirty, sixty and a hundred times what was sown. Although the parable makes the point that these various types of soil symbolize the various conditions of the human heart and its receptivity to the word, it nevertheless culminates with the assurance that the seed *will* produce a harvest. Despite the wastage along the way, "the dreary fallow land grows a field of waving corn, with a yield that surpasses all prayer and understanding. In spite of every failure and opposition, from hopeless beginnings, God brings forth the triumphal end which he had promised."[54] So, in spite of everything, there is an assured harvest. In the setbacks along the way we must remember the assurance of this final outcome, and the pastor–teacher must notice that the one who "hears the word of God and *understands* it" (13:23) is the one who bears fruit.

The next parable about growth in this chapter also has its downside. It is the Parable of the Weeds among the Wheat (13:24–30), and considering Matthew's focus on the nature of the Church in his Gospel, it is no surprise to find it here, although the field in which wheat and weeds grow side by side is not necessarily the Church, but the world, according to Jesus' own interpretation (13:38). Matthew is the only Gospel writer to include this parable, with its note of caution about the Church. The parable itself is simple enough. Among the good wheat, tares are sown, as if by an enemy (13:25,28). The Greek word for the tares is "*zizania*", and these weeds are probably the plant *Lolium temulentum*, a weed related to ryegrass. At first it looks like wheat, but then it turns out to be a weed. Its grains are poisonous and, if mixed with the good wheat, it makes the crop valueless.[55] The issue raised in the parable is whether the landlord's workers should go and dig out the weeds straight away (13:28). The landlord's reply is "No", since in digging up and gathering the weeds, the wheat will be uprooted as well. Sorting out the weeds from the wheat must occur only at the harvest time; until then, patience is required.

Like the Parable of the Sower, the Parable of the Weeds and the Wheat is given a separate explanation by Jesus (13:36–43). This is in strikingly Jewish language, recalling the apocalyptic vision of the Son of Man in Daniel 7. Until his judgement, weeds and wheat will grow side by side in the world. No judgement will occur until the end of time, when the Son of Man will send his angels to harvest both, separating and burning the weeds whilst gathering in the wheat (the righteous) who, to change the metaphor, "will shine like the sun" (13:43).Whether the parable is applied to the world or to the Church, the principles remain the same. It is not impossible to suppose that the Church could be sown with weeds that look like wheat, but turn out to be poisonous. To create a pure Church on the basis of human judgement could be very disruptive. The need for patience is paramount in the process, with the knowledge that the Son of Man will oversee judgement at the end of time.

Alongside these two growth parables, which have assured endings but conflicted processes, there are two others with unhindered growth at their heart. These are the Parables of the Mustard Seed and of the Yeast or Leaven (13:31–33), and they give further clues as to the nature of growth in the kingdom. The parables of the Mustard Seed and Yeast or Leaven have a single overarching message. Their meaning is that out of "the most insignificant beginnings, invisible to human eyes, God creates his mighty kingdom, which embraces all the peoples of the world".[56] The mustard seed, whether or not it is actually the smallest seed, grows into a large, if not the largest, of garden shrubs. Black mustard (*Brassica nigra*), which is grown in Palestine for oil and used as a condiment, can become as tall as five metres. The main point is simply the contrast between the planting of a tiny seed and its growth into a large shrub that can shelter many birds. In that respect there are echoes of Daniel 4:12,20–21, in which the Babylonian Empire is able to shelter many nations in its branches. Likewise, the kingdom of God, starting from the most insignificant beginnings—a baby born in an outhouse in Bethlehem, will eventually fill earth and heaven, with every tribe, nation, people and language finding rest and salvation in its branches (Revelation 7:9).

If the Parable of the Mustard Seed contrasts the size of the seed with the great result of giving shelter to many, the Parable of the Leaven or Yeast has the same dynamic, but with a slightly different twist. Once again, a very little yields a formidable result, as the whole dough is affected by the yeast. A Palestinian woman would generally use some of the sourdough from a previous baking to leaven the next loaf. The effect of the parable is the same as the Mustard Seed, and in the case of the leaven, everything in the bread is affected. Yet it is the nature of yeast that it is hidden throughout the dough. Here is a slightly different twist: the presence of the kingdom, although affecting all it comes into contact with, is hidden from view; it is a secret working, but that working is evident in the result.

Summarizing the four parables explored so far, we have seen that two of them, the Sower and the Weeds among the Wheat, stress the final harvest that is assured despite the difficulty of the process. There will be wastage. There will be opposition. A clutch of conditions in the human heart can prevent fruitfulness, as outlined by the different soils in the Parable of the Sower. The other two parables, of Mustard Seed and of Leaven, highlight the extraordinary growth of the kingdom.

Why did Jesus use parables at all? A considerable part of the chapter is spent on their rationale (13:10–17,34–35). According to an editorial comment by Matthew, the use which Jesus made of parables is, once again, in fulfilment of prophecy (13:35). Here the quotation is not from Isaiah, like so many others, but from the Psalmist Asaph: "I will open my mouth in a parable: I will utter dark sayings from of old." Thus, for Matthew, Jesus' teaching in parables is a fulfilment of a prophetic part of a Psalm in the Old Testament. There are also other reasons for using parables, which Jesus himself gives.

When the disciples come to ask Jesus why he speaks in parables (13:10), he draws a distinction between the knowledge given to them and what is given to the crowds. "To you it has been given to know the *secrets* [or mysteries] *of the kingdom of heaven*, but to them it has *not* been given" (13:11, NRSV, my italics). From this it seems that there are two groups around Jesus in his ministry: the disciples or apostles who have constant access to him, to his thoughts and actions; and the crowds. This is a practical matter: a large, popular group could not have the same access to Jesus as the small, hand-picked group of apostles. These disciples are therefore privileged. So there are "insiders" and "outsiders", but the boundary is not set hard. In fact, those who might have been categorized as *outsiders* find themselves *insiders*; for example, the centurion (8:10), the Samaritan woman at the well (John 4), and the Syro-Phoenician or Canaanite woman (15:21–28), to mention just a few. Meanwhile, those thought to be *insiders*, like the scribes and Pharisees, find that they are on the *outside* of the truth of the parable. Their hearts have no room for the seed. They do not understand, hence they do not grow spiritually. While the distinction between the apostles and the crowd is that the former are privileged with greater explanations as to the mysteries of the kingdom, and with that knowledge comes greater responsibility, the crowd can nevertheless listen carefully and grasp the reality the parables describe.

Jesus now gives two insights into revelation: the first is a kind of operating principle within the kingdom (13:12), while the other is a description of the outcome of spiritual truth as described by Isaiah (13:14–15). First, Jesus appears to be saying that distribution of understanding and gifting in the kingdom will not be equal. As in the Parable of the Talents, each has something, but some have far more than others! Again, in the Parable of the Talents (which we shall come to in a later chapter) some are given five talents, some two and some only one. Likewise, in the Parable of the Sower, there will be a varied response, even amongst the fruitful. Therefore neither spiritual gifting nor natural talents are ever equally distributed. The point here is that, depending on *how* we use what we are given, we may still get either more or less, so that it is possible for someone with much to end up with even more, and for someone with little to end up with nothing. It is not a question of this being predestined, but that our own response to the opportunities we are given will affect the result.

The second example, taken from Isaiah, seems at first reading, and for that matter at the second, very bleak. The words Jesus quotes here were spoken by a seraph to Isaiah at the time of his call, described in Isaiah 6. The prophetic task Isaiah had been given was to deliver a message to the people, to which they would not listen, however it was put. This was not so much an intention as a prediction. The point of sending Isaiah was, surely, to dissuade the people from going after false gods, and to persuade them to repent and be delivered. But the seraph, speaking on behalf of God, gave here the conclusion rather than the workings of the people's response. They would hear, but not comprehend. They would look, but not understand. The effect of this hardening in response to Isaiah's message was that their minds would be dulled spiritually, their spiritual eyes shut and their ears closed (Isaiah 6:10). This would occur as they rejected Isaiah's message, so that their state after hearing it would be more hardened than at the outset. To say that this was God's intention with no opportunity for repentance, rather than a prediction of the outcome, would be to undermine the purpose of the prophet's ministry, which was to bring about change. It would also confuse the result with the intention. For change was the purpose of God's appeal through Isaiah: "Come now, let us reason together," said the Lord. "Though your sins are like scarlet, they shall be as white as snow" (Isaiah 1:18). In using this quotation, Jesus is saying that the outcome of the parables is to provide opportunity for people in the crowd to discern spiritual truth and the mysteries of the kingdom, but that failure to listen and to heed his teaching will only lead to a further hardening of the heart. Parables, therefore, are a means of communication that invite engagement with the story they revolve around. For some, they have the effect of beckoning in, while others they shut out. The reason for this varied response must lie in the condition of the heart and mind of the listener. An example is given at the end of this chapter (13:54–58), where Jesus is rejected by those closest to him, his neighbours and acquaintances in Nazareth. In their case, familiarity with Jesus prevents them from listening to his teaching or drawing the right conclusions from his miracles. Their eyes are closed and their ears stopped, but this shutdown is caused by their own prejudice (Isaiah 6:10).

Finally, in this chapter Matthew gives us three quick-fire parables or sayings about the kingdom of heaven, showing principally the value of the kingdom and the judgement that lies in its wake. The first two parables, the Treasure and the Pearl, show the value of the kingdom (13:44–46). Although the message of each is fundamentally the same, the details of the stories are different. In the story of the hidden treasure, the discovery is accidental, while the exceptional pearl is found only after a long search.

These two methods, or ways of discovery, admirably illustrate the spiritual search. Some find true faith in Christ after a long and winding road of spiritual exploration, involving experiment and intellectual examination; others simply stumble upon it through a chance conversation, a sudden encounter, or a moment of illumination or epiphany. Whatever the means of discovery, the outcome is the same in each parable: complete commitment and sacrificial action to secure what has been discovered, for both people sell everything to obtain it, and in so doing are filled with joy (13:44). In both enquirers there is also complete determination to possess what they have found: the pearl merchant sells all his other pearls to buy the pearl of great price, and the farmer hides the treasure in the field until he can round up his assets and buy the land. The point is that the kingdom is so valuable, it is worth sacrificing all else to obtain it.

The third of these short parables (the Fishing Net) shifts the focus back to the idea of judgement, rather like the Wheat and the Weeds. The point is the same, even though the story is different. Wheat and tares are familiar to the cereal farmer; sorting the catch is familiar to a fisherman. There are about twenty different types of fish in the Sea of Galilee, and the law only permits the eating of fish "with fins and scales" (Leviticus 11:9–12). Other fish—like eels or catfish, plentiful in Galilee—have to be discarded.[57] Likewise, at the end of time the angels will sort out the evil from the righteous.

As a conclusion to this section, Matthew includes Jesus' question to the disciples about whether they have understood these parables (13:51–52). They simply, and perhaps blandly, respond, "Yes" (13:51). Taking them at their word, Jesus then instructs them *how* they are to teach in the future, comparing them to true scribes or teachers who are to bring out, as it were, new and old from their storehouse in order to provide for family or guests. The implication appears to be that the disciple (the true scribe or teacher) must draw on what is old and new: in other words, teaching from the law and the prophets *and* Jesus' own teaching on the kingdom. The Gospels often describe what Jesus brings as new wine (9:17; John 2:10). This new wine is to be produced along with the old, if it is in keeping with the kingdom. It is up to the true scribe to do this and, by extension, to produce the right food for the right occasion. For if the disciple understands, he or she will be fruitful (13:23).

Jesus began by teaching the crowds beside the lake (13:1), moving into a house to teach the disciples (13:36); now he goes to his home town where he faces rejection (13:53–58). This marks a break between one section of the Gospel and another. Commentators see five such sections, a parallel to the five books of the Torah. This is a prelude to what will follow. The ministry of Jesus in Galilee is drawing to a close. He has fulfilled Old Testament prophecies about his ministry in Galilee. He has healed and taught with great authority: many have been restored and large crowds taught and fed. The disciples and crowds have had long discourses of teaching. The shadow of the future will shortly fall over him: firstly in the death of John the Baptist, and then in his own prediction of his coming death and resurrection, following Peter's confession that he is the Christ. These themes are the bridge to the final part of Jesus' ministry.

CHAPTER 8

Jesus and John the Baptist

Matthew 3:1–12; 11:1–19; 14:1–12

One of the themes running through the early part of Matthew's Gospel is the relationship between Jesus and John the Baptist. We know from Luke that Elizabeth and Mary are cousins (Luke 1:36). Jesus and John the Baptist are therefore blood relatives and almost exact contemporaries, since their mothers—Elizabeth and Mary—are both pregnant at the same time (Luke 1:41–42). John also fulfils Old Testament prophecy, because he is "a voice of one calling in the desert, 'Prepare the way for the Lord, make straight paths for him'" (Isaiah 40:3; Matthew 3:3). John's call to repentance, expressed and symbolized in baptism, and in light of imminent judgement, sets the context for Jesus' own ministry.

Although these details are similar to the account given by the Jewish (but Romanized) historian Josephus in his *Antiquities of the Jews*, Josephus makes no reference to John's connection to Jesus.[58] Instead, John is described by Josephus as a very significant prophetic figure who "proved to be sufficiently influential to pose a more serious threat to Herod Antipas than apparently Jesus ever did".[59] The descriptions in the Gospels tend only to see John as a forerunner to Jesus, as he himself claims to be (Matthew 3:11), whereas Josephus depicts him as a "unique and distinctive representative of the Jewish prophetic tradition who deserves a prominent place in any account of the religious history of Palestine in the first century".[60]

John's ministry consists of three features, which Matthew makes clear at the outset: his style or asceticism, his preaching and the baptism that he administers, both in terms of its purpose and its limits.

John, we are often told, comes in the spirit of Elijah. Indeed, there is an expectation in the Old Testament that Elijah will come again before the Messiah appears (see Malachi 4:5). Jesus himself refers to this (Matthew 11:14). Many think Jesus is Elijah returned (Mark 6:15; 8:28; Matthew 16:14; Luke 9:19; John 1:21), especially after John is executed. Elijah was probably the greatest ascetic prophet of the Old Testament. He lived outside the centres of population, and during the great drought brought on by Elijah's prayer of judgement against Ahab for worship of Baal, was fed by the ravens at the Brook Cherith (1 Kings 17:1–6). No wonder that the Carmelite order, which gave rise to mystics like John of the Cross and Teresa of Avila in sixteenth-century Spain, found inspiration from Elijah.

Similarly, John has the profile of an ascetic prophet. We are told by Matthew, as indeed by the other Gospel writers (Mark 1:6, for example), that his clothes are made from rough camel's hair. He has a leather belt round his waist. He eats locusts and wild honey. We tend to skate over this diet, so familiar has the phrase "locusts and wild honey" become to us, but a pause for thought makes us realize it was the extreme diet of a complete ascetic. His example galvanized the desert-dwelling ascetic movement of the fourth and fifth centuries, especially in Syria, Egypt and Palestine.[61] This asceticism undoubtedly gave John standing in a period when the Qumran community, eschewing the world for the desert, lived their own self-denying existence by the Dead Sea.

John's preaching is a match for his asceticism. He thunders out of the desert to castigate the authorities of his day (3:7–10). No one escapes his strictures, whether Sadducees or Pharisees. The Sadducees were the elite leaders of Judah: defenders of the temple and strongly Hellenized. From their number the high priests generally came. As a religious party, the Pharisees emerged around 150 BC, in the time of the Maccabees, to withstand the forced Hellenization of Judaism by the Seleucid kings, notably Antiochus IV. They later made themselves the guardians of the Jewish law, imposing heavy burdens of conformity upon the Jewish people. The Pharisees and the Sadducees dominated the Sanhedrin—the Seventy—who formed the ruling council of Judaism in Jerusalem. Again and again in the Gospels they appear as opponents of Jesus, of his teaching and his actions.

Both groups, Sadducees and Pharisees, come down to the Jordan to enquire who John the Baptist is (John 1:19–28). He denies being the Christ, Elijah or "the Prophet" (see Deuteronomy 18:15–18). John is, instead, "the voice of one calling in the desert, 'Make straight the way for the Lord'"(Isaiah 40:3). To these elite religious leaders he says, "You brood of vipers! Who warned you to flee from the coming wrath? Produce fruit in keeping with repentance" (Matthew 3:7–8). The theme of John's preaching to these religious leaders is impending judgement: "The axe is already at the root of the trees, and every tree that does not produce good fruit will be cut down and thrown into the fire" (3:10). In light of this, the only true way forward is repentance leading to fruitfulness. There is no point in the Jews pleading their ancestry as children of Abraham, since God can raise up children of Abraham from the very stones (3:8–9). No, the only way forward is repentance, and the only entry point to a fruitful life is baptism.

The baptism that John administers is both a sign of repentance and a preparation for what is to come. Whereas John baptizes with water, Jesus will baptize with the Holy Spirit and with fire (13:11): fire being not only a metaphor for cleansing and judgement, but also for the presence of the Holy Spirit (see Acts 2:3, where the Spirit descends with "tongues of fire"). Sometimes people do feel a sense of heat today when the Holy Spirit rests on them. The coming of Jesus with the Spirit will not only empower his disciples but will be a sign of the judgement to come, of which Jesus will speak in the Parable of the Wheat and the Weeds.

John's imprisonment

This early description of John's baptism and preaching in Matthew's Gospel sets the scene for his ministry. The next time we hear of John (4:12) he has been imprisoned by Herod Antipas, also called Herod the Tetrarch, for criticizing him—and, more especially, his new wife, Herodias. She has divorced her first husband of many years, Herod Antipas' half-brother Philip (also called Herod II), in order to marry her brother-in-law. Both men are sons of Herod the Great by different wives. In doing this, Herodias has broken Jewish law as *she* initiated the divorce herself, probably under the auspices of Roman law, and is thus especially culpable. Herod Antipas, Herodias' new husband, has *also* previously been married: to Phaesaelis, daughter of the Nabatean King, Aretas IV, whose capital was at Petra. Between them they have had two divorces and have now married each other, breaking the Jewish law of consanguinity (Leviticus 18:16; 20:21). For his criticism John is imprisoned at Herod's fortress Machaerus in Perea, part of the district of Galilee. This appears to happen early on in the narrative of the Gospels (see Luke 3:19–20).

It is from this prison that John sends some of his disciples to ask Jesus the seemingly curious question (given John's earlier certainty), "Are you the one who was to come, or should we expect someone else?" (11:2–3). It is an odd question, since only a matter of months before, John has shown complete confidence that Jesus is indeed the Messiah, and the one who will baptize in the Holy Spirit (see John 1:29–34). The question implies that John now has some doubt that Jesus really is the Messiah, and these doubts have come to the fore in prison.

The reality is that prisons are places where doubts or negative thinking can quickly develop. Two things characterize life in prison: the incessant waiting in limbo and the reality of doubt. On 5 April 1943 Dietrich Bonhoeffer was imprisoned in the military section of Tegel Prison in Berlin. He would remain in various prisons until his eventual execution on 9 April 1945, when he was only thirty-nine years old. Implicated in a failed plot against Hitler, his days were numbered. Although blessed with a remarkably hopeful disposition, supported by a confident theology and trust in God, he nevertheless admitted how hard it was to get up in the morning. He went on:

> It is a queer feeling to be so utterly dependent on the help of others, but at least it teaches one to be grateful, a lesson I hope I shall never forget. In normal life we hardly realize how much more we receive than we give, and life cannot be rich without such gratitude . . . My time is always occupied, but in the background there is always *a gnawing sense of waiting for something to happen.*[62]

At least Bonhoeffer had a Bible, something to write with, the love of family and a fiancée (whom he would never marry), and above all he had the full story of Christ's life.

For John the Baptist, conditions and circumstances are very different. The life and ministry of Jesus is still in the making, and the conditions in the Machaereus fortress are as harsh or harsher. For John, those conditions and the "gnawing sense of waiting for something to happen" take their toll, precipitating his question to Jesus which springs from doubt: "Are you the one who is to come, or should we expect another?" (11:3).

That John should need reassurance, given his circumstances, is no surprise; that he has doubts as to the exact identity of Jesus shows the stress he is under. "Are you the one who is to come, or should we expect another?" is certainly very different from the exclamation, "Look, the Lamb of God, who takes away the sin of the world!" (John 1:29). A confident announcement has turned into a tentative question seeking reassurance. This is the work of doubt. Doubt is the flip side, the shadow side, of faith. There is, of course, more than one kind of doubt. There is the settled doubt of the sceptic, but even the sceptic doubts because he or she believes something. Then there is the doubt that comes from confusion, as the ancient Chinese riddle puts it: "If, when I was asleep, I was a man dreaming I was a butterfly, how do I know, when I am awake, that I am not a butterfly dreaming I am a man?" This is not the kind of doubt besetting John the Baptist. His doubt about the identity of Jesus is to be contrasted with his previous confidence and certainty. The conditions of his imprisonment, his physical distance from Jesus, or his isolation, and the inner workings of his mind and emotions have placed him in two minds, it seems, which is the classic description of doubt.

He needs the reassurance of hearing evidence that Jesus really is the Messiah. Just as Elijah, despite the amazing outcome of the contest with the prophets of Baal on Mount Carmel, gave way to dark thoughts of spiritual isolation and depression that made him despair of life itself (1 Kings 19), so too John, in his prison cell in Herod's fortress, needs to hear that his life's work has not been in vain: hence this loaded and hopeful question. Doubt of this kind is wrapped up with our emotions.

Os Guinness calls it a *"coup d'etat"* from within.[63] It is not wilful or wicked, but rather a form of human weakness in which our emotions and our physical condition create dark forces within:

> Out-voted, out-gunned, faith is pressed back and hemmed in by the unruly mob of raging emotions which only a while earlier were quiet, orderly citizens of the personality. Reason is cut down, obedience is thrown out, and for a while the rule of the emotions is as sovereign as it is violent.[64]

It is such doubt, created by depressed emotions or even despair, as with Elijah, that can send us—like Christian in *The Pilgrim's Progress*—into the dark dungeons of Doubting Castle. Such emotionally driven doubt can carry out a kind of blitz on our belief, but faith is the art of holding on to things our reason has already accepted, in spite of our changes of mood. Who knows what mood has settled on John in the fortress of Herod, isolated and frustrated as he is? He thus sends two or more of his disciples to Jesus with the vital question.

Jesus is not offended at being asked by John the Baptist if he is the Messiah, or whether John should look for another (11:3). As with Simon Peter on the beach of Lake Galilee in John 21, when Jesus recommissions him following Peter's denial, there is no recrimination. Jesus' response is practical and helpful for a man whom he greatly admires, and who is facing suffering and possible death. He replies to John's messengers, "Go back and report to John what you hear and see: the blind receive sight, the lame walk, those who have leprosy are cured, the deaf hear, the dead are raised, and the good news is preached to the poor" (11:5). In other words, Jesus is doing those things prophesied of him by Isaiah (Isaiah 35:5–7; 61:1–3) and which John will himself recognize as being prophetic of the Messiah's actions.

Once again, evidence as to who Jesus really is stems from the fulfilment of prophecy. Fulfilment of prophecy is the heartbeat of the Gospel, proving that Jesus is the Christ. The evidence is incontrovertible, as so many in Galilee have received healing and teaching from him. To hear this from his messengers must have been immensely reassuring for John. Often those facing crises in life need the pastoral reassurance of the well-foundedness of their faith in Christ, mediated through the comforting presence of a Christian friend.

As the messengers take the reply from Jesus back to John, Jesus turns to address the crowd (11:7–19). With lilting oratory, he exalts John's ministry. In a series of rhetorical questions he narrows down the true estimation of John. John is not a popular orator matching his words to what the people want to hear, bending to others' behests—a reed shaken in the wind. Far from it. He is not a privileged elitist bedecked in fine clothing. He could not be more different from that, covered as he is only with animal skin, and eating a diet of honey and locusts. No, he is a prophet, and more than a prophet. No one is greater than him. He is the one foretold by Malachi who will prepare the way of the Lord (Malachi 3:1; Matthew 11:10). In fact, says Jesus, if you can accept it, he is an Elijah to the nation, in the manner of the first Elijah, reawakening Israel to true faith in an era of apostasy (11:14). John is one of those who forcefully advances the kingdom of heaven in this era (11:12). Yet despite such a build-up, Jesus surprisingly says that *anyone* who lives in this new era of the kingdom is *greater* than John. They are greater in the sense that they enjoy greater privileges and opportunities than John could ever do, simply because of his place in salvation history. For all his greatness and dedication to the kingdom which he is ushering in with Jesus, he essentially belongs to the Old Covenant, and is executed before Jesus' full inauguration of the New Covenant through his death and resurrection.

Having praised John to the crowd, Jesus now criticizes them. They cannot be satisfied. They are perverse. The crowd is like children calling to other children in the market place: "We played the flute for you, and you did not dance; we sang a dirge, and you did not mourn" (11:16–17). Just so, John comes with a sombre message of repentance and is accused of having a demon. Jesus, contrastingly, comes to feast and joins in people's parties and is accused of being a glutton and a drunkard, "a friend of tax collectors and 'sinners'". You can't win.

Sometime later John is executed in extraordinary circumstances (14:1–12). Herodias, Herod the Tetrarch's second wife, nurses a deep resentment against John for his criticism of her marriage to her brother-in-law. In Jewish law, Herodias' marriage to Herod is illegal, as marriage to a brother-in-law is proscribed. Then her daughter Salome pleases the court so much with her dancing on Herod's birthday that Herod rashly promises her any request, up to half his kingdom (14:6–7; Mark 6:22–23). As we know, Salome asks her mother what she should request of the king, and Herodias suggests that John the Baptist's head be brought to the feast on a platter. How grotesque is revenge!

Despite Herod's distress at such at a request, he does not want to lose face in front of his dinner guests by withdrawing his rash promise, so the execution goes ahead. John the Baptist's head is duly brought into the feast on a platter. It is an unspeakably sordid, vindictive, tawdry and malevolent act, and has been the subject of countless works by great artists, including Caravaggio's *The Beheading of St John the Baptist*. Caravaggio painted the scene of the execution with Salome standing by with a golden platter, ready to receive the head. This picture now hangs in St John's Co-Cathedral in Valetta, Malta. Caravaggio painted a further two pictures showing John's head on the platter: one, all too vivid, which hangs in the National Gallery in London, and the other in the Prado. For John to have lost his life in such a base and ignoble way reinforces the cruelty of bitter enmity.

It is not surprising that the disciples of John, having first buried his body, go to tell Jesus of his death (14:12). When Jesus hears, he understandably seeks solitude and time for reflection (14:13). He does not immediately get it. The crowds follow him, in need of teaching, healing and food. Only after meeting those needs, and once he has dismissed the crowd and sent the disciples on ahead of him, does Jesus have time to pray alone (14:23). No doubt the subject of his prayer is not only lamentation for John's end, but also his own forthcoming Passion. It is only a little later that Jesus begins to prepare his disciples for his own execution. John's beheading is a shadow which now falls over Jesus' life, reminding him that his own crucifixion is not far away. This is an important step along the way of Jesus' fulfilment of what has been planned from eternity. It is also a powerful signal to Matthew's Jewish readers that the cost of discipleship is never far away.

CHAPTER 9

The Watershed of the Gospel

Matthew 16:13–28

The watershed in Matthew's Gospel comes soon after the news of the death of John the Baptist (14:13–36). Following that grim message, Jesus seeks solitude, is followed by a large crowd, teaches, then feeds the five thousand, and walks across the lake to the struggling disciples who have spent about nine hours rowing or sailing across the sea. Peter briefly ventures outside the boat and tries to walk on water, but after a few steps he sinks beneath the waves and is immediately rescued by Jesus (14:22–33). A debate ensues between Jesus and the Pharisees about ritual cleansing, which we shall return to in Chapter 11, "Mercy, not Sacrifice". A further retreat north to the region of Tyre and Sidon yields a meeting with the Syro-Phoenician woman. Her feisty and witty conversation results in the healing of her daughter through Jesus' power (15:21–28). After further time spent around Galilee teaching, healing and feeding the hungry (15:29–39), as well as further confrontations with the Pharisees and Sadducees (16:1–12), Jesus takes his disciples to the furthest point north recorded in the Gospels: to Caesarea Philippi (16:13), for what will be the pivotal moment in Matthew's account.

The Synoptic Gospels (Matthew, Mark and Luke, so named because they share common material, synoptic being derived from the Greek words for "with" and "view") divide into two parts. The first part— approximately half of each account—focuses on the ministry of Jesus in the region of Galilee and the underlying question, "Who is he?"

The second halves of these Gospels focus on what Jesus has come especially to do, beyond the extraordinary works of power and the teaching that he gives in the region of Galilee, which in turn demonstrate

93

the kingdom of heaven. His identity and his mission are encapsulated in the conversation that takes place in Caesarea Philippi. It is the watershed of each Synoptic Gospel. It ends the period of joyful teaching and ministry in Galilee and begins the journey to Judea, over which falls, increasingly, the shadow of the cross. A physical watershed often has green, lush vegetation on one side, where plenty of rain falls, while on the other side, where there is low rainfall, one finds scrubby vegetation, rocky terrain and fewer signs of life. The confession of Simon Peter at Caesarea Philippi is just such a watershed; the ministry in Galilee, with its joyful exuberance, is over, and the progress to the cross now begins, with increasing tension and a sense of foreboding.

Although there have been several previous recognitions of Jesus as Messiah in the Gospels, Caesarea Philippi proves to be where the *definitive* identification of Jesus as the Messiah and God's Son takes place. Some of the earlier confessions come very early in the ministry of Jesus, even at the outset. In other Gospel narratives, John the Baptist recognizes Jesus as the Lamb of God who has come to take away the sin of the world, and the one who will give the Spirit (John 1:29,33). Andrew has also recognized Jesus as the Messiah from the beginning (John 1:41). Nathanael makes a spontaneous confession: "Rabbi, you are the Son of God; you are the King of Israel" (John 1:49). Yet despite this initial acclaim, Jesus now looks for a considered, collegiate, and definite response from all his disciples as to who he is. Nothing else will do.

When the disciples have assembled with him at Caesarea Philippi, Jesus puts his vital question to them; it comes in two stages. First he asks *generally*, "Who do people say the Son of Man is?" (Matthew 16:13). This is phrased using the now familiar third person, with Jesus referring to himself as the Son of Man, his favourite self-designation. It is a title drawn from the writings and visions found in Daniel 7, where Daniel records:

> In my vision at night I looked, and there before me was one like a son of man, coming with the clouds of heaven. He approached the Ancient of Days and was led into his presence. He was given authority, glory and sovereign power; all nations and peoples of every language worshipped him. His dominion is an everlasting

dominion that will not pass away, and his kingdom is one that
will never be destroyed.

Daniel 7:13–14

By now the disciples are familiar with Jesus' use of this title and self-
designation, but they still have to link it with another great Old Testament
figure found in Isaiah: the suffering servant (see Isaiah 42:1–9; 49:1–13;
50:4–11; 51:16; 52:13–53:12). The disciples answer Jesus confidently,
telling him that most people put him firmly in the category of a prophet.
He is either John the Baptist revived, Elijah who is expected to return to
Israel, having left earth without dying (2 Kings 2:11–12; Malachi 4:5–6),
Jeremiah or another of the prophets. All these designations fall short of
the truth. As if indicating that this is an inadequate answer, Jesus presses
the disciples further for *their* response: "But what about you? Who do
you say I am?" (16:15).

How long a pause there is before Peter replies we do not know. As if
to underline the formality and the pivotal nature of this conversation,
Matthew gives Peter his full name, Simon Peter; he confidently asserts,
"You are the Christ, the Son of the living God" (16:16). It is a twofold
answer—the Christ, the Son of the Living God—to what is originally a
two-part question that moves from the general to the personal. Peter is
the spokesperson for all the disciples.

The first part of Peter's answer acknowledges that Jesus is "the
Christ". "Christ" comes from the Greek "*Christos*" and is the equivalent
of the Jewish title "Messiah", meaning the "anointed one". Although not
specifically mentioned as a title in the Old Testament, the term has its
roots in the kingship of David and the prophecies of Isaiah.[65] By the first
century, a number of expectations had coalesced around the title, so it
carries with it a number of fervent hopes for the nation. The Messiah will
be a descendant of David, of the royal line, and thus the Son of David.
He will unite Israel and its twelve tribes. He will restore the nation to its
rightful sovereignty and independence, and he will restore the temple.

Whenever the term "Messiah" was used by a first-century Jew, it
carried with it these expectations. Jesus will do these things, but in a
different way, and with very unexpected results. He will create one new
nation of Jew and Gentile (see Ephesians 2:11–22; 1 Peter 2:4–10), which

is his body, the Church. Jews and Gentiles will be united in Christ. The temple will be restored, but it will not be the physical building, destined for destruction and obsolescence, but instead it will be Jesus' body raised from the tomb (see Matthew 26:61; 27:51; Mark 13:1–2). It is this disconnect between the popular understanding of what the Messiah will come to do and what Jesus has in fact come to achieve, and the means by which he will do it, that makes Jesus swear the disciples to secrecy when they rightly confess him to be the Messiah (16:20). Otherwise this widespread misapprehension about the Messiah will lead to Jesus being restricted by, or entangled in, the false messianic expectations of popular understanding.

There is, then, a paradox in Jesus' acceptance of the title "Messiah": on the one hand he is glad of their acknowledgment of his calling, but on the other he warns the disciples against advertising the fact, because of popular misapprehension.

If the first half of Peter's answer is that Jesus is the Messiah, the second part is that he is the "Son of the living God" (16:16). King David was originally designated a son of God (that is, treated as though he were a son; see 2 Samuel 7:1); this title did not imply divinity of any kind, but simply that God would treat David with fatherly care and discipline. And the Qumran community, a first-century Jewish monastic community living by the Dead Sea, who had a strong eschatological expectation (looking firmly towards the end of all things) and were waiting for the coming of the Messiah, believed their own prayer and purity would hasten his coming. For them, as for the Pharisees, a connection is made between the Messiah and Psalm 2, in which God says, "You are my son; today I have become your father" (Psalm 2:7). Qumran also made the connection between the Messiah and God's son.[66] Peter's declaration linking the Messiah with the "Son of the living God" is foundational—there can be no Christianity without it. The participle "living"—added here as a prefix to "God"—is only rarely used in the New Testament (about a dozen times), but it conveys a powerful dynamic. On the one hand, God would not be God if he were not living, but it is also "a powerful reminder that the God with whom Jesus is here being connected is not a philosophical abstraction but the dynamic God of Israel's faith and history".[67]

Peter does not make this confession or receive this insight from a sojourn in Qumran (of which he may not even have heard), nor from extensive study of the Scriptures (Old Testament). One imagines he would only have had the rudimentary knowledge of the Scriptures of a fisherman, unlike the years of study needed to become a teacher of the law like a scribe or a Pharisee. But by now Peter has spent perhaps a full two years in Jesus' company, has seen vast crowds, countless miracles and extraordinary teaching. And from what Peter knows, both from common expectation and from attendance at synagogue, Jesus can only be a prophet or more than a prophet.

Through the impulse of the Holy Spirit and his own observation, Peter acknowledges Jesus as Messiah. Straight away Jesus puts this down to divine revelation: "Blessed are you, Simon son of Jonah [or John], for this was not revealed to you by man, but my Father in heaven" (16:17). Flesh and blood have not given Peter this insight, but divine revelation. He is blessed, but he is to be further honoured.

One declaration by Peter, that Jesus is the Messiah, gives way to another by Jesus, that Peter is to be the "rock" (16:18); they are reciprocal declarations. Jesus assigns Peter a nickname, given and recorded at an earlier stage in John's Gospel (John 1:42), but in Matthew much more is said. Peter's nickname is reminiscent of the occasions in the Old Testament where names are changed: Abram becomes Abraham; Sarai becomes Sarah; and Jacob becomes Israel. In each case, the new name speaks of the vocation or calling of the individual; thus Abraham means "father of many nations", while Israel means "struggle". Peter means "rock": "*petros*" in Greek, "*petrus*" in Latin, or in Aramaic, "*kēpā*" ("Cephas", KJV). This reminds me of the habit in Uganda where, in the Rutori language (spoken in the Toro kingdom in the western part of the country), everyone is given a nickname from a choice of about twelve words that depict character. Each nickname describes a type of person: carer, helper, teacher or leader.

Simon (whose name means reed) is to become a rock. This is his journey, from a reed to a rock: from someone who bends in the strong gales of opposition to someone who, in time, becomes a rock in the Church. Jesus goes on to say that Peter will *personally* be the rock on which the Church will be built (16:18). Those who reject the primacy of Peter and his successors believe that what Jesus *really* means here

is that Peter's confession (that Jesus is the Christ) is the rock, bulwark
and foundation of the Church, rather than any individual. Such a gloss
on Jesus' words does not appear to be what Jesus is actually saying.
Arguably, Jesus may not be envisaging the primacy of the Bishop of
Rome in perpetuity, but he certainly gives unique authority to Peter
in the Church during his lifetime. And Peter's immediate successors
from earliest times, including Linus (2 Timothy 4:21), Anacletus and
Clement, all first-century Bishops of Rome, are acknowledged as leaders
of the Church, although the full panoply of the papacy is based on an
uneasy mixture of biblical claim and fabricated fact—the Donation of
Constantine, for example, a forged document supposedly authorized by
the Emperor Constantine in the fourth century, giving Bishops of Rome
supremacy in the Empire. However, it is upon Peter's ministry that the
"*ekklesia*" ("church") will be built, and nothing will prevail against it;
this is evident in the early chapters of Acts, where we see his address and
leadership at Pentecost (2:14–47), his inclusion of the Samaritans (8:14),
his initial leadership of the church in Jerusalem (5:3–10) and, above all,
his welcoming of the Gentiles into the Church through God's powerful
prompting (chapters 10 and 11).

Peter, as we see in these passages, is given "the keys of the kingdom"
(Matthew 16:19). He is given authority to prohibit or permit teaching or
activity in the church. Peter will discover that his teaching and actions
do not always have divine endorsement, but he is given divine guidance
"to enable [him] to decide in accordance with God's already determined
purpose."[68] Nevertheless, from such an exalted calling, Peter falls almost
immediately, showing how his rock-like qualities are embryonic rather
than solid, his nature still more reed-like than rock-like! For within a
matter of minutes, Jesus has as gravely rebuked Peter as earlier he has
so graciously exalted him. In a trice Peter has become a stumbling block
rather than a rock.

Now formally acknowledged by his disciples as the Messiah, Jesus
begins to explain what the Messiah has principally come to do and what
it will involve. In a dramatic change in the narrative, presaged by Matthew
with the phrase, "From that time on . . .", Jesus begins to speak about his
calling and how "he must . . . suffer many things at the hands of the elders,

chief priests and teachers of the law, and that he must be killed and on the third day be raised to life" (16:21).

These words mark the end of the comparatively carefree Galilean ministry, and the ominous journey to Jerusalem begins. Although, as we see in John's Gospel, Jesus' ministry in Galilee is punctuated by visits to Jerusalem for the "appointed festivals", expected of every male Jew (see Leviticus 23; Deuteronomy 16:1–17), for the most part Jesus resides and ministers in Galilee until this moment when, having been confessed as the Messiah, he sets his face like flint to go to Jerusalem (see Luke 9:51). Matthew now encapsulates this journey to Jerusalem, where Jesus will enter the city for his Passion and give final teaching on the future of all things (16:21—20:34). These chapters comprise further revelation as to the identity of Jesus—the transfiguration—and teaching about living in the new Christian community. First, Peter must come to terms with Jesus' future.

On hearing Jesus' predictions, Peter takes it upon himself to rebuke such pessimistic thinking. The Messiah, he thinks, cannot suffer in this way. "Never, Lord!" says Peter. "This shall never happen to you!" (16:22). In speaking like this, Peter reflects the general view of the Messiah in the Judaism of his day. The Messiah is to be a national liberator, as already noted. It will not be until after the resurrection, and during the fifty days between what we now call Easter and Pentecost, that Peter will come to understand that the Messiah is to be delivered up "according to the definite plan and foreknowledge of God" (Acts 2:23, NRSV). Peter does not realize what Jesus knows, namely that the Messiah will combine in himself the twin vocations of two great Old Testament figures: the Son of Man and the suffering servant. If the picture of the Son of Man, as we have seen from Daniel, is one of infinite power and majesty, the picture of the suffering servant in Isaiah is one of complete abandonment and rejection (Isaiah 53:10), suffering vicariously for our salvation (53:3–5), and taking the punishment due to us upon himself (53:6).

In Jesus are combined suffering and victory, abandonment and exaltation, sin-bearing and satisfaction for sin (Isaiah 53:11). Peter can accept the majestic vision of the Messiah coming as powerful liberator, but not the idea of a Messiah who is rejected by his own people and who suffers a humiliating execution on a Roman gibbet. For Peter, such an end is a disaster to be averted at all costs. In other words, there is as yet no place in his vision of the Messiah for the suffering servant. He therefore rails against Jesus' prediction that he will be killed at the express demand of Israel's leaders. Drawing Jesus to one side, Peter rebukes him strongly for such talk. Little does Peter know of the express plan of the Father to offer his Son as a willing, eternal sacrifice for sin, as an expression of his love, as an example of innocent and unjust suffering, and as victor over the devil and death. However, he will eventually preach this at Pentecost (Acts 2:22–36).

Without Jesus going through the agony of crucifixion, none of this can be achieved, but to dissuade him from suffering this death is to do the devil's work—hence Jesus' unusually sharp response. He traces Peter's reluctance to let him face his destiny back to its evil source and says, "Get behind me, Satan! You are a stumbling block to me; for you are setting your mind not on divine things but on human things" (16:23, NRSV).

Finally in this section, Jesus calls his disciples to the same self-sacrifice:

> "If any want to become my followers, let them deny themselves and take up their cross and follow me. For those who want to save their life will lose it, and those who lose their life for my sake will find it."
>
> *Matthew 16:24–25, NRSV*

These words may not have made much sense until after the crucifixion, when "taking up a cross" would have had vivid and compelling meaning. The phrase has become a metaphor for giving up our lives in the service of Christ and in so doing finding life. This is admirably illustrated by Jim Elliot in his famous words, "He is no fool who gives what he cannot keep, to gain what he cannot lose."[69] Killed by Huaorani Indians in Ecuador in 1956 as he sought to reach them with the gospel, Elliot exemplified this conviction. His wife Elizabeth bravely continued his work, and Jim's life became an inspiration to thousands.

After his formal recognition as the Messiah by the disciples, even if they do not understand what this involves, Jesus sets his face to fulfil his destiny as the Lamb of God who has come to take away the sin of the world (John 1:29). His ministry now moves from Galilee to Judea.

The imperative of fulfilling his predicted destiny takes hold of Jesus' life. He must fulfil what is said about the suffering servant in Isaiah, as well as receiving the honour of the Son of Man prefigured in Daniel. On two further occasions in Matthew's Gospel Jesus warns the disciples of what is to come (20:17–19; 26:2,31–32). Yet they do not comprehend his warnings until after the traumatic events of their Lord's Passion and crucifixion. His sacrifice is the only way by which Jesus will gather around him a new community, the Church, at the centre of which is faith in a crucified and risen Lord. By fulfilling what had been planned before the foundation of the world, as Peter came to understand (see Acts 2:23–24,32; 1 Peter 1:18–20), a new community is formed in which Jew and Gentile can become one. It is to Matthew's compilation of Jesus' teaching about the life and values of this new community that we now turn. This teaching is one of the hallmarks of the Gospel and is the fulfilment of God's mysterious plan (see Ephesians 3:1–12).

CHAPTER 10

God's New Community

Matthew 10, 17, 18 and 19:1–20:16.
(If you are using this book as a group, see p. 163 for
more ideas of how to approach this section.)

More than any other Gospel writer, Matthew appears to lay down the
principles and disciplines for developing and leading the Church. In
that sense, his seems to be more self-consciously a Gospel for church
membership and leadership than the others. Mark is principally focused
on announcing the good news and the kingdom to the public; Luke
demonstrates that the kingdom is for the outsider;[70] and John's Gospel
is a considered statement of the significance of the Word being "made
flesh" (John 1:14). Matthew not only shows how Jesus fulfils everything
promised in the Old Testament—from the law and the Prophets to the
role of Davidic kingship—but also provides comprehensive teaching on
what it means to be a member of this *new community*, the Church. The
teaching begins with instructions, first given to the apostles by Jesus, on
how to make the kingdom known to others (10:5–42). The names of the
twelve apostles are listed (10:1–4), then their immediate task is outlined:
an extension of Jesus' own ministry in Galilee, healing the sick, delivering
those who are demonized and preaching the kingdom (10:7–8).

Matthew 10

The principles of mission in Matthew 10, laid down by Jesus for the apostles, are—by extension—for the whole Church. Only later will the intended audience of the apostles' preaching and ministry be widened from the narrow focus on the "lost sheep of Israel" (10:5–6) to encompass "all nations" (28:19). As we know from Acts 1:8, the followers of Jesus will go to the Samaritans and the Gentiles, and then into all the world. In Matthew 10, Jesus goes on to explain the task of the apostles, the conduct expected of them and the challenges they will face. The essential core of their mission will be to announce the nearness of the kingdom to those they meet, and to demonstrate its presence by a number of actions.

The message is the same today: "The kingdom of heaven is near." This is an announcement similar to Paul's message to the Athenians in Acts 17, in which he says that God "is not far from each one of us"; then, quoting from the classical poet Epimenides of Crete, Paul adds, "For in him we live and move and have our being" (Acts 17:27–28). The point is the same today: neither the kingdom of heaven nor the presence of God is far from any one of us. He is, in fact, as close as the genuine prayer that seeks forgiveness and reconciliation. This message is therefore one of great hope and encouragement. It is up to the apostles to announce this to those whom they meet (10:7). The mighty works they are called to do in Jesus' name are similar to his own: "Heal the sick, raise the dead, cleanse those who have leprosy, drive out demons" (10:8). In other words, give hope.

In 2012, a friend and I went to Egypt and spent a few weeks in and around Cairo, both at a monastery near Cairo called St Macarius the Great, and at Coptic churches in the city. One of the most memorable of these churches is the Zabbaleen community's worship space in Mokattam village in south-west Cairo, which is a cave church hewn out of a rock face. Zabbaleen literally means, "rubbish people". Their livelihood comes from collecting rubbish around the city and, where possible, recycling it. Among this Coptic community churches have been planted, miracles have taken place, care and community have been established, and each week Jesus is made known in word and sacrament in the cave church amidst the rubbish. Thousands are being blessed and taught in this most unlikely of places. The kingdom of heaven is indeed among them. Theirs are faces of joy in forgotten places. They continue the ministry of the apostles.

Not only does Jesus tell the apostles what to do in terms of their preaching and actions, but he also tells them how to go about it—what their conduct is to be. They are to travel light. If the Son of Man has nowhere to lay his head, "his representatives can expect no material security except in God".[71] Money is not needed, as hospitality is expected en route. They can take a pack ("*pēra*") with them, in which food can be carried. The prohibition against spare clothes and sandals shows an additional form of asceticism, which the discalced (without shoes) orders of Carmelites followed in sixteenth-century Spain, as did John of the Cross. Lastly, in terms of equipment, they are not to take a staff or walking stick, although Mark suggests they can (Mark 6:8). Some feel the need to harmonize this discrepancy with the other Gospel accounts, whereas others can live with variation in the Gospels, without calling into question their veracity, inspiration or authority.[72] Since the apostles are travelling light, they will be dependent on finding people whom Jesus describes as "worthy" (Matthew 10:11) to offer them hospitality. Such a welcome will be provided because of Middle Eastern hospitality laws towards travellers, but also because the apostles are intrinsically "worthy of their keep" (10:10). Examples of such hospitality are frequent in biblical literature: in Genesis, for example, in the account of three angels visiting Abraham (Genesis 18:1–8). This visitation, generally accepted to be by the Trinity, is famously captured by the icon painter Rublev in his well-known and much-loved icon depicting the hospitality shown by the Trinity.

These instructions given by Jesus focus on the need for simplicity and faith. Our church youth group leader recently arranged a similar challenge. A group of five young people agreed to take part in a spiritual exercise. They arrived at a pre-arranged airport to travel to an unknown destination, which turned out to be Switzerland (not the cheapest country in Europe). They took barely any money with them, thereby depending on the hospitality of strangers they met. In fact, they quickly met some locals with whom they could share their faith and with whom they spent two nights. The exercise was modelled on these instructions of Jesus, and it was doubtless an experience the young people will never forget.

In the more distant past, the itinerant ministry of the mendicant Friars, beginning with Francis of Assisi, had great influence in Europe in terms of evangelism and spiritual counsel, until the ownership of property dented their initial zeal and effectiveness.

Furthermore, Jesus says there is to be an exchange of blessing with those who receive the apostles into their homes: "As you enter the home, give it your greeting. If the home is deserving, let your peace rest upon it; if it is not, let your peace return to you" (10:12–13). The disciple or apostle is to be an effective channel of peace to that home, both the building and the people in it. After moving recently into a new house, and building a rather lovely extension study, I asked a friend to come and bless the space, so I could begin to use it for writing and for teaching preparation. He readily agreed, and about twenty of us gathered in the room to pray for God's blessing on this place. I have no doubt that this prepared it as a place of study and writing for God's work; the atmosphere was set and established. One recent visitor even said she felt the power of the Spirit as she entered the room!

The transmission of peace is something Jesus expected. This pronouncing of blessing may have been neglected in evangelism in the past, but it is more readily understood today. The ministry of blessing is integral to making known the kingdom.[73] An offered blessing may be either received or rejected (10:13–14). If received, such an action could be the first step in receiving salvation. If, on the other hand, one of God's representatives is not welcomed and is positively rejected, judgement is released on that household or community, with potentially serious effects (10:14–15).

After giving the apostles instructions about how they are to conduct themselves on this mission, Jesus now warns them about their vulnerability: "I am sending you out like sheep among wolves. Therefore be shrewd as snakes and as innocent as doves" (10:16). This is a prelude to Jesus pointing out that opposition and persecution will come, not only from the authorities in society, but also from a disciple's own home or family. Jesus gives this warning to the apostles before a final piece of sobering encouragement.

Persecution might come from either the local synagogue or a disciple's family, or both. Local Jewish councils, comprising twenty-three officials, could hear cases breaching Jewish by-laws and customs. They could inflict punishments, either physical or financial, on those deemed at fault. Proclamation of a false Messiah, as the synagogue labelled Jesus, could result in severe punishment or even stoning (see Stephen's martyrdom described in Acts 6 and 7). Others could be hauled up before governors or kings, as would happen to the apostle Paul during his long imprisonment in Caesarea (see Acts 24–26). When this happens, Jesus says, the apostles can be assured of the Holy Spirit's help (10:16–20), just as the Spirit will help Peter before the Sanhedrin (Acts 4:8–13), giving him and John boldness and power in argument.

Unlike Luke and John, Matthew rarely mentions the work of the Holy Spirit. In this rare mention, the Spirit's work is reserved for support in times of persecution. Words of power and assurance will be given to the disciples in those situations, taking away any natural fear or trepidation. The Spirit will speak through a disciple—as in the cases of Stephen, Peter, John and Paul in Acts, when they find themselves in front of magistrates or rulers.

If persecution comes through civic authorities, whether Jewish or Roman, it will also come, more disturbingly, from members of a disciple's own family: "Brother will betray brother to death, and a father his child; children will rebel against their parents and have them put to death" (Matthew 10:21). It is a grisly picture, further highlighted by Jesus' later teaching in the same chapter that he will bring division into a family, setting "a man against his father, a daughter against her mother" (10:35). Bleak though it may be, it nonetheless happens, especially when commitment to another religion—such as Islam—is overthrown by a new-found faith in Christ. Christians from countries such as Iran regularly find themselves in fear of their lives because of their Christian allegiance, and sometimes undertake the gruelling journey to the West to find asylum. Many have trodden that risky route. I have met some and honour their courage—not a few have found their way to churches in England.

Jesus, grimly but realistically, warns of what has since become all too true, that "a man's enemies will be the members of his own household" (Matthew 10:36). Facing such persecution, the disciple will simply be following in the steps of Jesus, for "a student is not above his teacher", in this as in other respects. If Jesus is insulted and attacked physically, so too will his followers be (10:24–25). Yet they are not to be afraid, since in the hour of their testing, or when they appear in court to answer charges, they will be given words to speak by the Holy Spirit. This is what happens, as we have noted, when Peter and John find themselves in front of the Sanhedrin, on trial for healing a crippled beggar at the temple gate called Beautiful (see especially Acts 4:8–12).

The warnings that Jesus gives the apostles when he sends them out are realistic and sobering, but nonetheless we know from other Gospel writers who record the return of a wider group of seventy-two disciples from a similar mission that their joy is far greater than any duress they suffer (Luke 10:17–24). So in spite of the serious warning that Jesus has given the twelve, he concludes his teaching with added motivation for mission and reasons for *not* being afraid. Fear can be crippling, but Jesus mentions a number of reasons why they should not be afraid. Although his teaching may for a time seem to be hidden or concealed, it will be made obvious later, and "shouted from the rooftops" (10:26–27). Thus the truth of what Jesus says will become apparent. Secondly, it is far more important to obey Jesus and his Father than to give in to fear of the opposition orchestrated by those who can only "kill the body" (10:28). This is the martyr's choice, which would become normal during the first three centuries of Christianity in the Roman Empire. Such martyrs looked beyond their physical suffering to a reward in heaven. Furthermore, our heavenly Father knows both when a sparrow falls to the ground and the number of hairs on our head, so nothing escapes his attention or his care. Such knowledge is a comfort in our discipleship: at the very least, Jesus knows. Finally, a disciple is a representative of Christ and his kingdom. He carries with him his master's authority and should receive a welcome as though he were his master. Anyone who welcomes a disciple—that is, "a little one"—will receive a reward. Such support will not go unnoticed or unrewarded (10:40–42).

In these ways Jesus prepares the apostles for mission and for extending his kingdom, which is also the means of extending the Church. Conduct in that church is what Mathew now turns to after some intervening teaching and actions that conclude Jesus' ministry in Galilee. If Matthew

10 is all about principles of mission, Matthew 18:1—20:16 is mostly about the conduct of relationships in the church.

Instructions for church life: Matthew 17, 18, 19, 20:1-16

The Church is the new community that Jesus comes to found, containing both Jews and Gentiles; indeed, in time it will encompass every nation, tribe, language and people. In this section, Matthew provides instructions to pastors on how to conduct relationships in this new community. Earlier, in Matthew 17, Jesus has been depicted fulfilling the law and the prophets by appearing during his transfiguration with both Moses (the law) and Elijah (the prophets). At this summit meeting, Jesus is transfigured before his inner circle of disciples: Peter, James and John. His glory overwhelms them. The Father speaks of his love for the Son, and the subject of the conversation between Jesus, Elijah and Moses is Jesus' "exodus" or departure (Luke 9:30–31).

On the way down the mountain Jesus and the disciples meet a frustrated parent whose son the disciples cannot heal (Matthew 17:14–21). The remaining disciples, who have not been with Jesus on the Mount of Transfiguration, are not yet ready to restore a demonized boy subject to seizures: their faith is insufficient, their urgency in prayer too lacking (17:20 and Mark 9:29). Later in the same chapter Jesus appears to indicate and anticipate the obsolescence of the temple and its unfair and burdensome imposition of tax through the indirect way in which he and Peter pay the temple tax. Payment is made through a fish which has the required sum of money in its mouth (17:24–27). It is as if, unwilling to pay the tax, Jesus summons it from the deep.

The discourse of Matthew 18:1–20:16

The Church is to be a new community with humility at its heart; the temple will be replaced, and healing will be part of the Church's mandate from the start, together with a new set of radical standards. Jesus sets about outlining the principal values of the Church, and the new standards it should embody.

At the beginning of this discourse about the Church, Jesus talks once again about humility. The discourse about relationships, particularly in the Church, matches the other discourses in Matthew (see chapters 5—7, 10, 24 and 25) and has the same significance. Humility is a consistent theme in this Gospel (see especially 11:28–30). The fact that the conversation between Jesus and the disciples in chapter 18 centres on humility and comes at the *start* of this section is telling, and anticipates Augustine's words that humility, humility and humility are the first, second, and third most important qualities in a Christian.[74] Jesus explains by answering the disciples' all too self-seeking question, "Who is the greatest in the kingdom of heaven?" He more than surprises them by bringing a child into their midst and pronouncing, "I tell you the truth, unless you change and become like little children, you will never enter the kingdom of heaven. Therefore, whoever humbles himself like this child is the greatest in the kingdom of heaven" (18:3–4). Jesus could not be clearer: we are to be childlike. Anyone who abuses one of these little ones will be severely judged, with a millstone hung around the neck of the offender who will then be cast into the sea (18:6). In this case, "little ones" refers to children, whereas elsewhere in the Gospel "little ones" can also be a diminutive or nickname for disciples (18:6,10,14). Furthermore, those who do things that cause others to sin will be judged (18:7). It is better to cut off or cut out offending members (hands, feet or eyes) than to be led by them into grave sin (10:8). The actual words are a Hebraism or manner of speech underlining the gravity of what is being said. Any loss is preferable to the whole person going into "*gehenna*" (the place where Jerusalem's rubbish was burnt, but used figuratively by Jewish writers to mean "hell", the place of ultimate punishment). The discourse thus begins with startling teaching on both humility and self-discipline. It continues with an appeal to restore the wandering sheep, or disciple.

After a reminder of the worth of each disciple, whose personal angel in heaven sees "the face of [the] Father" (18:10), it is no surprise to hear the Parable of the Lost Sheep, which demonstrates the care of the Father for his "little children". Interestingly, whereas Luke uses this parable to show the Father's care for the *lost*, culminating in the Parable of the Prodigal Son (Luke 15:1–32), from a different editorial perspective Matthew uses it to show the pastoral heart of the Father in going after a wandering disciple (18:12), and in personally bringing him or her back to the fold. Matthew's use of the parable is therefore pastoral, while Luke's is evangelistic.[75]

The discourse now turns to settling disputes in the church and to forgiveness. The earlier section (18:15–20), dealing with the settling of error, is followed by a section dealing with the forgiveness of someone who has offended us personally (18:21–35). Anyone who knows church life knows that these two issues are vital for a healthy and harmonious community life. In relation to settling a matter where someone has been sinned against, Jesus lays down a strict sequence of settlement to be followed in a church. It can be seen as dealing with an infringement of the church's or another's legitimate rights through increasing circles of publicity and so loss of reputation. If someone has been slandered, offended, robbed or humiliated by another member of the church, then he or she is firstly to go *privately* to the individual and, hopefully, be reconciled. If that person listens and offers an apology or restitution, or both, the matter is settled. If the person will not listen and refuses to make amends, then the offended party may take two or three witnesses to help bring about a settlement, following Old Testament law (Deuteronomy 19:15). If the person still will not listen or be reconciled, then the whole church may be told of the fault, and if that makes no difference, the offender may finally be cast out of the fellowship (surely the basis of excommunication). Having established this process, Jesus vests authority in the collective decision-making of the church. In verses 18 and 19 the word "you" is plural, and refers to the way the church may either permit (loose) or prohibit (bind) decisions of faith or conduct. Once again, this presumably lays the basis not only for local decision-making but also for the Catholic (meaning universal) Church Councils, which took place from Nicaea (325) to Chalcedon (451). The foundation of this authority appears to be the presence of Christ, often invoked through prayer: that is, when two or three are gathered together in his name, Christ is present (18:20).

Having spoken about discipline and reconciliation, it is no surprise that the discourse, as arranged by Matthew, should move on to forgiveness. This teaching is prefaced by a brief conversation with Peter (18:21–22), who asks Jesus, "How many times shall I forgive my brother when he sins against me? Up to seven times?" In saying this Peter has already gone beyond Rabbinic expectations which suggests three times. But Jesus answers radically, not seven times, he says, but seventy times seven. In other words, there is no limit to forgiveness.

To reinforce the thinking behind this teaching, Jesus tells the story of a king forgiving a subject a vast debt of ten thousand talents, which is a staggeringly huge sum (18:23–35). Having been shown such generosity and mercy, the subject then insists that a fellow servant who owes him the comparatively paltry sum of one hundred denarii—although this was still over three months wages for a labourer—must pay it all. When the second man fails to do so, the first, having initially tried to strangle his debtor, has him thrown into prison. This action is reported to the king, who chastises the first by saying, "Shouldn't you have had mercy on your fellow servant just as I had on you?" The logic is unanswerable, especially given the scale of the first man's debt. The lesson from the parable is clear: "This is how my heavenly Father will treat each of you unless you forgive your brother from your heart" (18:35). Forgiveness is not an option. It is a command and duty, however difficult a process it might be.

Mercy, forgiveness, reconciliation, discipline and humility were—and are—to be marks of the Church. In Matthew's compilation of his teaching, Jesus now moves on to describe family relationships, and then the power of grace in motivating Christian service and distinctiveness.

The discourse continued: family life (Matthew 19:1–15)

This chapter or sequence in the Gospel begins with Matthew's formula for concluding the previous section. Thus he writes, "When Jesus had finished saying these things, he left Galilee and went into the region of Judea to the other [east] side of the Jordan." Although this saying marks a geographical break from what has gone before, and is the start of a new section of teaching, there is nevertheless enough consistency with the preceding passage to treat them together. Jesus is teaching about the radical new values of the kingdom of heaven, and about the church community which should both illustrate and point towards that kingdom.

Firstly, Jesus deals with the issue of divorce in reply to one of the many questions he is asked by Pharisees and Sadducees in this Judean stage of his ministry (see also 22:23–33,34–40 and 41–46). Jesus' reply gives him the opportunity to teach about marriage. The context of the question is the dispute between the two rabbinic schools led by Shammai and Hillel respectively (see also the comments on divorce in chapter 4).

The Hillel view of divorce was the more liberal one, interpreting the Mosaic rule of Deuteronomy 24:1–4 to mean that a man might divorce his wife if she "displeased" him. Such displeasure could amount to anything: from untidiness around the house, infertility, poor cooking, to adultery. Any such reason would, in Hillel's estimation, be grounds for divorce. By contrast, Shammai permitted divorce for one reason only: adultery. Presumably most Jewish husbands preferred the former interpretation, giving them easy divorce opportunities. In this context, Jesus—as a leading and popular teacher—is asked for his opinion, and as with many such questions, stands to lose popularity or respect with his answer.

Before answering the question, Jesus first refers back to the institution of marriage, and in so doing, gives us an insight into his understanding of the law that has both primary and secondary levels of importance within it. He shows us that the Deuteronomy passage is about a pragmatic provision for dealing with a problem that has arisen, namely the "indecency" of the wife.[76] Yet there is a more determinative passage governing marriage in Genesis 1 and 2. Jesus looks at the original principle of marriage from the biblical account of creation, and argues that this "original principle must take precedence over the later concession to human weakness".[77] This principle is that marriage should be unbroken. Male and female are combined in marriage to become one flesh, and "what God has joined together, let no one separate". In other words, divorce was not envisaged at the inception of marriage. Furthermore, Jesus himself attributes this teaching or description of marriage not just to Moses—the human author of Genesis—but to the Creator, or God himself (19:4–5).

"What, then, is the purpose of the Mosaic rule in Deuteronomy?" object the Pharisees (19:7). Jesus replies that it is provision for human hardness of heart, but was never the Creator's intention. He then goes on to say that only on account of adultery may there be divorce, thus siding with Shammai in the dispute between the rabbinic schools. The disciples are shocked by such a ruling, and respond that in that case, it would be better not to marry (19:10), presumably revealing that their thinking is more on the side of Hillel's teaching. Taking the disciples at their word, Jesus admits that not everyone will be able to "accept this word" (referring to his teaching), meaning that his high standard for marriage and divorce will not be acceptable to all and that, as the disciples have hinted, not everyone will want to go into marriage on such a basis.[78]

Finally, Jesus says that some will not be called to marriage: they have "renounced marriage because of the kingdom of heaven" (19:12). They will choose celibacy. This will not be for all, but some may choose it and others will reluctantly live with it. From the third century onwards the Early Church made celibacy an important part of discipleship, as did Origen, the Cappadocian Fathers, Augustine and Jerome, but in fairness, Jesus never said celibacy was a better way of life, only that some are gifted for it.

If Jesus' teaching about marriage and divorce is radical, his attitude to children also surprises the disciples. In keeping with what Jesus has already taught (in Matthew 18:1–6) about who is the greatest in the kingdom, when he placed a child among the disciples and called him or her with childlike trust the greatest, Jesus now once again welcomes children as exemplars of the kingdom (19:13–15). The disciples should know better than to prohibit parents from bringing little children for him to bless. He rebukes the disciples and praises the children, saying the kingdom of heaven belongs to them. In effect, he gives them a vital place in the kingdom and in the new community he is creating. Marriage and family are building blocks, together with celibacy, in the life of the new community: each can give to the other something that complements their life.

Grace, wealth and rewards (Matthew 19:16–20:16)

The teaching now shifts to faith and rewards. A young man from the elite of society, in possession of great wealth, approaches Jesus, recognizing him to be a rabbi or teacher. This is also a man who is earnest and spiritually ambitious. Yet from the outset the conversation is not easy. In Luke's version (18:18), the rich young ruler addresses Jesus as "Good teacher", making Jesus' riposte in Matthew to his opening question a little easier to understand: "Why do you ask me about what is good? There is only One who is good" (19:16–17). Immediately Jesus seems to be raising the bar for this rich young man by talking about the perfection of divine goodness. He may have discerned that this was the kind of thinking in which the young man dealt. To the challenge from Jesus that he should obey the commandments, the young man says he has kept them all from his youth. The young ruler's almost blithe response may demonstrate that, while he might not have broken the commandments in deed, he may not have applied Jesus' more rigorous teaching on the law to his *thought life* (compare 5:17–30). The man still wants to attain perfection, however, so Jesus answers him in his own terms by saying, "If you want to be perfect [*"teleios"*], go, sell your possessions and give to the poor, and you will have treasure in heaven" (19:21). Such a demand is more than the young man can cope with, so he goes away sorrowfully. He possesses, we are told, "great wealth".

The issue arises as to whether Jesus' command to this man is a universal requirement of salvation. The answer from the New Testament overall must be that it *isn't*, for when Peter is asked on the day of Pentecost, "Brothers, what shall we do?" his answer is "Repent and be baptized, every one of you, in the name of Jesus Christ for the forgiveness of your sins. And you will receive the gift of the Holy Spirit" (Acts 2:37–38). Repentance and faith are the irreducible minimum for reception of the Spirit. However, "sanctification" (the process of becoming more like Jesus after initial justification) involves not only keeping the commandments, but also following the call of God in our lives, and in some cases taking vows (or commitments) of poverty, chastity and obedience, as very many in the early years of Christianity—and since—have done. Many of the early Fathers made this their aim, including Basil of Caesarea, Athanasius, Gregory Nazianzus and Augustine of Hippo.

If perfection for the rich young ruler requires selling up and following Jesus, it is not something he feels able to do. Nor, says Jesus, in explaining how difficult it is for the rich to enter the kingdom, can the wealthy easily do this either. Indeed, it is like a camel going through the eye of a needle (19:23–24). Only God's amazing grace can enable such a thing; only the experience of this grace can prise wealth from the grasp of the rich. Jesus concludes that what is impossible for human beings is possible with God. It is grace operating in the community of the Church that enables great acts of generosity and sacrifice.

The conversation now takes on a different twist with the interjection of Peter. In a rather crude way, Peter asks what others probably think but never voice: "We have left everything . . . What then will there be for us?" (19:27). Jesus does not rebuke Peter. He says that at the end of time there will be rewards for all who sacrifice property, wealth or family for Christ, a hundred times over (19:29). He then goes on to tell a concluding parable in this section about how this reward system will work. Once again, the teaching is full of surprises.

The Parable of the Workers in the Vineyard (20:1–16) is a classic parable of Jesus, along with the Prodigal Son, the Sower, the Good Samaritan, the Sheep and the Goats, the Pharisee and Publican, and the Marriage Feast. Such parables, maybe more than others, determine our understanding of the kingdom. The point about the Labourers in the Vineyard is summarized by Jesus at the end of the parable with the saying, "So the last will be first, and the first will be last" (20:16). Payment in the kingdom is not according to length of service, but according to the generosity or grace of the "owner". Reward is granted by grace and not by desert.

In the story, different groups of workers are hired by the owner for a denarius a day or "whatever is right", a denarius being the normal day's wage in Jesus' day. The owner hires workers at 6 a.m., 9 a.m., midday, 3 p.m. and lastly at 5 p.m.—just an hour before sunset. Normal practice would see people being paid in proportion to the hours they worked, and this would seem fair. Yet there is another form of fairness, which is that each is paid the sum offered by the owner, or "whatever is right"

(20:4). When payment comes at the end of the parable, naturally we would expect those hired first to be paid first, but not so. Equally, we would expect those who have worked for twelve hours to be paid twelve times more than those who have worked for only one hour, but again not so. On the principle of the owner's right to do what he likes with his money, and that none get less than a denarius, a normal day's wage, the owner is shown to be generous to all. When translated into spiritual terms, it means that the dying thief (Luke 23:42–43), who knew Christ for only minutes, is offered the same gift of eternal life as an apostle who has served a lifetime. They may have different responsibilities in heaven, but they both have the same right to be there: the entrance fee for all has been paid by Christ.

With this teaching, the section comes to an end: a discourse divided into two by the movement of Jesus from Galilee to Judea (19:1). Essentially, however, all this teaching is about the conduct of the Church, its values and motivation. Humility, pastoral care, reconciliation, forgiveness and mercy are the drumbeats of this new, eternal fellowship, the Church. Loyalty and inclusion of the vulnerable are to be badges of membership. Finally, God's grace will truly inspire generosity and sacrifice, and will be the source of our rewards in the future.

The discourse ends with another prediction by Jesus of his coming death and resurrection (20:17–19). On the way into Jerusalem he heals two men who are blind, like Bartimaeus (Mark 10:46–52), and who recognize that he is David's greater son (20:29–34). Once again Jesus explicitly teaches the disciples that "whoever wants to be first must be [their] slave—just as the Son of Man did not come to be served, but to serve, and to give his life as a ransom for many" (20:27–28). The story of that ransom-giving is about to begin in earnest with Jesus' entrance into Jerusalem. We return to this narrative in the final chapter of this book. For now we look at the prophetic teaching of Jesus and his final combustible judgement on the spirituality of the scribes and Pharisees, which has been simmering throughout the Gospel, but reaches boiling point in chapter 23.

CHAPTER 11

Mercy, not Sacrifice

Matthew 9:9–17; 12:1–14; 15:1–20; 16:5–12; 23:1–39

Throughout the Gospel of Matthew, as with the other Synoptic Gospels, there is a strong sense of the predictions of the Old Testament prophets being fulfilled by Jesus, both in his teaching and his life. Not only that, but Jesus makes use of the outlook of the prophets in his observations on contemporary Judaism. We have already noted, in the Sermon on the Mount, the law being fulfilled and extended in scope, from simply being about deeds to a concern with words and thoughts (Matthew 5:17–48). Indeed, the wisdom teaching present in the Old Testament is also fulfilled and extended in the teaching of the Sermon on the Mount (see especially 6:19—7:27). The use made by Matthew of the prophets is essentially twofold: firstly, the prophets' words predict the outline and detail of Jesus' life from birth to death and resurrection, thus demonstrating that he is truly the Messiah, and secondly, they provide a deep insight into true righteousness and the heart of God, his feelings and attitudes alongside the law.

The function of the prophets in the Old Testament is to challenge the faith of Israel, to warn of coming judgement unless there is change, to predict the coming of the Messiah—especially as Suffering Servant (Isaiah) and Son of Man (Daniel)—and to upbraid the community of Israel or Judah for departing from the precepts of the law.

If the law provides the standard God calls his people to live by, the prophets are the messengers of YAHWEH who point out the consequences of failing to implement that standard in their national life. Yet more than that, they express the emotion and the heart of God towards his people: his love, his longing (Hosea 14), his sense of hurt at being abandoned

(Isaiah 5:1–7) and his patience. Prophecies convey a sense of the feelings of God himself, alongside the cold stone of his commandments. They are the messengers of God's faithfulness, whether in judgement or salvation, who—in the end—promise a liberator to heal and deliver his people. Jesus comes to his people as Prophet, Priest and King: this is demonstrated and fulfilled, especially in Matthew's Gospel.

As king, he is Lord, having all authority (28:18), but his authority is meekly borne (11:29–30). As priest, he upholds and fulfils the law, but is also the ultimate sacrifice on behalf of his people. As prophet, he comes to tell those who only apply the law in burdensome ways that God looks for mercy, not sacrifice. Furthermore, Jesus comes to speak the truth prophetically, where others live in the half-light of self-deception or manipulation for their own power and financial self-seeking. As a prophet, Jesus comes into especially stark confrontation with the appointed guardians of the law: the scribes and the Pharisees. It is to these moments in the Gospel that we now turn.

Matthew 9:9–17

Here, in the context of the calling of Matthew himself, one of the great principles of Jesus' teaching in relation to his actions is enunciated. Jesus' ministry in Galilee is getting underway: the centurion's servant is healed, along with many others; Jesus calms the storm; two demon-possessed men and a paralytic are cured (8:1–9:8). Amidst this stirring activity, Matthew the tax collector—a despised profession—is called to follow Jesus (9:9–13). He does so, but before he begins his discipleship he throws a retirement party in his house, to which many other tax collectors and "sinners" are invited, as well as Jesus and his disciples. When the Pharisees see this they ask the disciples, "Why does your teacher eat with tax collectors and 'sinners'?" The answer Jesus gives is drawn from the teaching of the prophets. It also reflects "similar proverbial sayings [which] occur in several Greek writings",[79] such as, "It is not the custom of doctors to spend time among people who are healthy, but where people are ill,"[80] Jesus says, in reply to the Pharisees' objection, "It is not the healthy who need a doctor, but the sick" (9:12). In other words, it should be no surprise that Jesus, a spiritual doctor and saviour, should be found among those who need him most. But more than that, he tells the Pharisees to go away and consider what Hosea meant when he said, "I desire mercy, not sacrifice" (Hosea 6:6). Jesus will quote these words again, a little later in the Gospel (12:7).

Hosea, whose name means "He saves", was an eighth-century prophet in the Northern Kingdom which, by then, had prostituted itself before innumerable idols and Baals (Hosea 11:2). The sadness for YAHWEH was that the more he called them back to himself, the more Israel sacrificed to Baals. Yet what God wanted from them was not their ceremonies, their liturgies, and their interminable feasts with no moral consequence. No, what God desired was hearts full of mercy (the Greek word "*eleos*") and steadfast love (the Hebrew "*hesed*"), not the performance of ritual duties with hearts that were far from him. How often the prophets of the Old Testament said this or something similar. As Isaiah put it:

> When you spread out your hands in prayer, I will hide my eyes from you; even if you offer many prayers, I will not listen. Your hands are full of blood; wash and make yourselves clean. Take your evil deeds out of my sight! Stop doing wrong, learn to do right! Seek justice, encourage the oppressed. Defend the cause of the fatherless, plead the case of the widow.
>
> *Isaiah 1:15–17*[81]

What God is looking for is not oft-repeated acts of religious ritual with no moral content and devoid of true compassion and mercy. Nor is he looking for ritual purity blind to the needs of others, but for acts of generosity, justice and kindness. Micah famously summarized this call as follows:

> He has shown you, O mortal, what is good. And what does the LORD require of you? To act justly and to love mercy and to walk humbly with your God.
>
> *Micah 6:8*

Thus, in relation to the type of company Jesus keeps (tax collectors and "sinners"), and with regard to the observation of ritual purity and the keeping of the Sabbath, the Pharisees should seriously consider, should go away and think about what "mercy, and not sacrifice" really means. This is the prophetic challenge that Jesus repeatedly throws down before the Pharisees and scribes.

The Sabbath and ceremonial washing (Matthew 12:1–14; 15:1–20)

We have already reflected on Jesus' dispute with the Pharisees over the correct use of the Sabbath (in chapter 6). As the Sabbath was given as a day of rest, it should be life-giving and a blessing (Exodus 20:8–11). In Mark's Gospel, Jesus encapsulates the purpose of the Sabbath vividly in the saying, "The Sabbath was made for humankind, and not humankind for the Sabbath" (Mark 2:27, NRSV). The Pharisees, on the other hand, have turned it into a legal nightmare. The number of prohibitions imposed on the Jews for the correct observation of the Sabbath turned it into a minefield, rather than a day of refreshing. Jesus and his disciples are criticized for gathering ears of corn and eating them on the Sabbath, and then Jesus is in danger of losing his life for healing a man with a withered hand (12:14). Once again, he tells the Pharisees to ponder the meaning of God's words through the prophet Hosea, "I desire mercy, not sacrifice" (12:7). Once again, in forgetting the purpose of the Sabbath, the Pharisees are life-denying rather than life-affirming. Once again, Jesus uses the prophetic injunction of Hosea to prevent a false use of the law.

A little later on in the Gospel Jesus is again in conflict with the Pharisees, although over a different subject. This time the conflict is about honouring parents and ritual washing (15:1–20). Once again, in this section Jesus looks for a right interpretation and handling of the law. What Jesus appears to be arguing for in this conflict is recognition of the underlying principles and reality of our discipleship, in relation to parents and to ritual washing. To understand why these two examples (parental care and ritual washing) come up together, we must trace the development of the argument.

The initial objection made by the Pharisees concerns the disciples of Jesus breaking the tradition of the elders by not washing their hands before eating (15:2). The underlying question here is how binding a tradition is, in comparison with an actual scriptural command. For although the Pharisees accuse the disciples of not following the tradition of the elders (ritual washing before eating), they willingly set aside a scriptural commandment to honour parents (Exodus 20:12) if it conflicts with a human tradition called "Qorban" ("devoted to God", Mark 7:11).[82] So the reason Jesus says to the Pharisees, "[Y]ou nullify the word of God for the sake of your tradition" (15:6), is because they set aside the commandment of honouring father or mother by this unrequired tradition of Qorban. It may flatter their sense of religious pride, but it does nothing to help needy parents.

Jesus takes the argument one step further when explaining this dispute to the disciples. He says, in effect, that ritual purity in itself—although an important part of Judaism—cannot in the end purify a person, for the problem is internal and not external. For the Jew, ritual purity revolves around keeping food laws, bodily cleanliness (for example, any body affected by a discharge must be cleansed by temporary separation from the community; see Leviticus 15), and keeping apart from the dead, from Gentiles, and from those who are unclean because of disease or sin. In addition, only certain "kosher" food can be eaten (Leviticus 11). The Pharisees devotedly attempt to keep all these rules, thus keeping themselves pure and separate. But whereas their emphasis is on the outer life and its purity, Jesus shows that his concern is for the inner life and its integrity and goodness. Jesus finds fault with the Pharisees and scribes, firstly because, although they attempt to keep all the ritual purity of the Old Testament regulations, their hearts, as Isaiah says, are far from God. Indeed, Jesus quotes the prophet in full, saying, "This people honours me with their lips, but their hearts are far from me; in vain do they worship me, teaching human precepts as doctrines" (Matthew 15:8–9, NRSV, quoting Isaiah 29:13). It is thus quite possible to go through all the motions while our hearts—our true affections and our true aspirations—are somewhere else. This is a continual challenge for all who are involved "professionally" in leading others in the spiritual life. We know what we should do, we know how to give the impression of doing it right, but all the while our hearts are somewhere else.

Not only does Jesus say that purity or integrity are a matter of the heart, but also that what makes us unclean is not prohibited food going into us, or our failure to wash, but unclean thoughts and actions proceeding from within us. In a classic observation of the nature of our humanity, Jesus says:

> "Do you not see that whatever goes into the mouth enters the stomach, and goes out into the sewer? But what comes out of the mouth proceeds from the heart, and this is what defiles. For out of the heart come evil intentions, murder, adultery, fornication, theft, false witness, slander. These are what defile a person, but to eat with unwashed hands does not defile."
>
> *Matthew 15:17–20 (NRSV)*

This perception amounts to a revolution. Jesus has offered a radical diagnosis of the human condition. External cleansing and external purity will not do. A deep cleaning of the heart so that it produces righteousness is what is needed. Such a deep clean is what Paul, a Jewish convert to Christianity, speaks about in Romans 7 and 8, where he finds in himself a law (or principle) tending to sin and death, from which he needs to be delivered, and finds the answer in the forgiveness of Christ and the power of the Spirit (see especially Romans 7:14–20 and 7:24–8:4). In effect, Jesus has fundamentally moved the goalposts of righteousness. Instead of believing that by rigorous observance of the law a person may become acceptable, one must acknowledge that external purity is quite insufficient. Only forgiveness and a changed heart, promised by the prophets (Jeremiah 33:8; Ezekiel 36:24–32), and new God-given aspirations from that changed heart will be acceptable.

The disciples must move on with Jesus, amazed once again (15:16). All the commonly accepted parameters of righteousness are being overturned. Matthew does not go as far as Mark, who in an editorial comment relating to this conversation says that Jesus "declared all foods clean" (Mark 7:19). Yet soon it will become clear that if what we eat is not important, and that it is where our heart is that matters, more than all the ritual washing or all the kosher food we have eaten, then keeping on eating in that kosher way will no longer be necessary. In fact, it could become a misleading snare. For a Jew this is revolution indeed. Once again it is not *sacrifice performed*, but *mercy received and given* that distinguishes the true disciple.

The wrong type of yeast (Matthew 16:5–12)

This little sequence is generally thought to be obscure. The conversation appears to arise out of a misunderstanding over Jesus' use of the word "yeast". The first misunderstanding is that the disciples, who seem a little unnerved, appear to have forgotten to bring any bread with them, and more than that, seem anxious about it! Jesus, who can be hard to understand when he takes a metaphor of common concern and turns it into a spiritual teaching, leaves the disciples uncertain. He already knows that the disciples have forgotten the bread and are thinking about it, but he makes a related point about the Pharisees' "teaching" being like unhealthy yeast. As if being rebuked for failing to understand the phrase "the yeast of the Pharisees and Sadducees" is not enough, Jesus goes on to say that they should not be worried about the absence of bread, since he has already provided enough bread for five thousand and four thousand people respectively. And on both those occasions there was much bread left over. At the very least they should have confidence in him to help them out of a tight fix when they have no food, but also they should be aware of the false teaching of the Pharisees, who promise bread which turns out to be like stone.

Returning to the symbolism of yeast, Jesus goes back to his original point that the yeast of the Pharisees and Sadducees is dangerous. That is to say, the religious teaching of both groups is pervasive and pernicious. Like a dangerous bacillus, it can incubate in religious communities and produce diseased results. What might this amount to? In the first instance, it could lead to a misunderstanding of the character of God: that far from being gracious, compassionate and full of steadfast love (see Exodus 34:6; Lamentations 3:22–23; Jeremiah 31:3), the God of the Pharisees' teaching appears as a hard taskmaster, a faultfinder, a peevish, pernickety, patriarchal figure. Such a view of God will only result in the diseases of fear, anxiety and neurosis. There is nothing in their theology approaching the lines of Faber's hymn, "There's a wideness in God's mercy like the wideness of the sea", nor of God's extravagant saying through Isaiah, "Come now, let us reason together . . . Though your sins are like scarlet, they shall be as white as snow . . ." (Isaiah 1:18). Rather, the God whom the Pharisees project, and who this yeast is like, is narrow, is unaffected by human suffering, and demands ever closer conformity to law with no hint of grace. If this yeast is bad, worse strictures on its efficacy and the mission of the Pharisees are to come, in Jesus' greatest piece of invective against them.

Condemnation of the Pharisees' spirituality (Matthew 23)

There are few more excoriating pieces of teaching in Jesus' ministry than in these verses in Matthew 23, where he denounces the Pharisees and the hypocrisy that they demonstrate. Once again we must remember that Matthew is a Jew, writing for predominantly Jewish churches in Judea or Syria, or both. So the strictures of Jesus on Pharisaic spirituality, which only Matthew conveys in his Gospel intended for Jewish Christians, are probably startling, giving his readers deep pause for thought. Earlier in the Gospel, during the Sermon on the Mount, Jesus has shown the bankruptcy of the spirituality of the Pharisees. He teaches a secret and selfless manner of spiritual devotion, in which there is privacy and brevity in prayer, anonymity in almsgiving, humility in fasting, and simplicity and honesty in speech. If Jesus, in the Sermon on the Mount, has lifted the cover on the Pharisees' hypocrisy (a word that literally means "play-acting"), he now blows it out of the water with a torrent of invective.

At the outset Jesus says of the Pharisees that although they "sit in Moses' seat" and should be listened to as they explain the law, they do not do what they claim to do—they do not practise what they preach (23:1–3). The effect of following their teaching is to have wearisome and heavy burdens imposed. And they do nothing to alleviate these burdens. Far from wanting people's freedom and lightness of spirit, the Pharisees seek only their own authority at the expense of their charges' guilt and anxiety. The purpose of the Pharisees' teaching is only to increase their own prominence and visibility in the community: they wear special clothes (phylacteries and tasselled prayer shawls; 23:5); they take the best seats at banquets and in the synagogues, and expect recognition in the marketplaces; they desire deferential and honouring treatment and want special forms of address, like "Rabbi" (teacher) or "father". In fact, the people have only one teacher, who is the Messiah or Christ, and only one Father, who is in heaven (23:8–10). The Pharisees love to accrue titles and honour to their name, which sets them apart and strokes their pride. Yet the greatest teacher will be a servant, for "All who exalt themselves will be humbled, and all who humble themselves will be exalted" (23:12, NRSV).

Jesus then proceeds with blazing prophetic force, with seven "woes", sounding like one of the prophets of the Old Testament (see, for example, Isaiah 5:8–23; Jeremiah 46–50; Ezekiel 35–39). "Woes" are essentially judgements against a community, a people, a group, city, nation or individual.[83] The *first woe* is a general condemnation of the outcome of the hypocritical instruction of those who teach the law: it shuts the entrance to the kingdom both to themselves and to others (23:13). The *second woe* shows the perverted course of their zeal. A zealot cannot be faulted for commitment, which carries them over sea and land to make a proselyte or convert, but the outcome of such zeal is in serious doubt: Jesus says to the teachers of the law and Pharisees that it makes the convert "twice as much a child of hell as you are" (23:15). In other words, such converts are burdened with a distorted fanaticism or extremism. A definition of extremism, in an age plagued by it, is the violent or fearful suppression of human wellbeing by a religious imperative. The *third woe* (which relates back to 5:33–37) is against the misuse or abuse of language, where simple, truthful speech gives way to a gradation of oaths. These oaths appear to lend more or less gravity and truthfulness to speech. Yet our words should not be linked to this casuistry, in which one oath is more important than another; instead, all speech should be truthful and self-evident, and no oath should be needed (23:16–22). The *fourth woe* is one of Jesus' most memorable sayings in his criticism of the Pharisees, and shows how a well-placed metaphor can surpass hundreds of words: "You blind guides! You strain out a gnat but swallow a camel" (23:24). The metaphor refers to an essential failing of the Pharisees in their teaching and spirituality: they became so myopic in their obedience to the law that they lost all sight of its purpose. "You give a tenth of your spices—mint, dill and cumin. But you have neglected the more important matters of the law—justice, mercy and faithfulness" (23:23). You should have observed both these requirements, says Jesus. That concentration on detail or the minutiae of life can make us lose the wider, more important, fundamental perspective of justice, mercy and faithfulness. It is a reminder that anyone can lose perspective through an overly narrow focus.

The *fifth woe* is a reminder of what we have already seen, which is that the spirituality of the Pharisees seizes on externals and neglects what is happening on the inside. They focus on the need for ritual washing (see 15:1–20), but neglect to cleanse the heart, the source of moral filth. Cleanse the heart, says Jesus, and the outer life will be clean as well (23:25–26). The same theme is carried through to the *sixth woe*, which recalls that the Pharisees eschewed the dead, giving them a wide berth for fear of ritual uncleanness; but here they are told that they are themselves like whitewashed tombs—another powerful metaphor—all white on the outside, with nothing inside but dust and dry bones, which are implicitly unclean and useless. Once again, they look good on the outside but conceal corruption within (23:27–28).

The final and *seventh woe* continues the theme of death, but now relates to memorials. This "woe" makes a new, yet more serious point. It is easy to give praise to those in the past who perhaps delivered a very uncomfortable message, but who are now silenced by death, and whose message has mellowed by the passing of the years. The Pharisees and the teachers of the law join in the praise of past prophets, but they show by their treatment of John the Baptist and of Jesus that they would have opposed the prophets of the past, whose tombs they now adorn. They are as spiritually bankrupt and as opposed to God as were their forebears (23:29–32).

All in all, the emptiness of the Pharisees is laid bare, and in doing this, Jesus proposes a different way of life and spirituality. Rather than adding burdens, he wants to bring rest; rather than bolstering speech with vain oaths, he wants us to season speech with salt and light; rather than suffocating our discipleship through a myopic concentration on detail, Jesus wants us to practise justice, mercy and faithfulness; rather than tending the outside of our lives only, he wants us to clean up the inside with his help; rather than applauding past radicals at a comfortable distance, he wants us to be in solidarity *now* with what the prophets stood for; and finally, rather than obscuring or shutting the entrance to the kingdom, he wants us mercifully to lead people into it. He desires mercy, not sacrifice.

A time is now coming, says Jesus, when a final chance will be given to Israel. Not only will Israel's spiritual leaders have the Messiah come to them (whom they will crucify), but others will be sent in the apostolic age: prophets, wise men and teachers. They too will be strenuously rejected, and so this generation will be more culpable than any other (23:34–36). If only Jerusalem and its leaders were willing to respond positively to Jesus: "How often I have longed to gather your children together, as a hen gathers her chicks under her wings, but you were not willing" (23:37). Instead, desolation has come (23:38), and will be completed in the future.

CHAPTER 12

Fulfilling the Future

Matthew 24 and 25

As we approach the final chapters of Matthew's Gospel, we find an intense focus on the future, in both the short and the long term. The teaching that Jesus gives here, alongside the gathering events and momentum of his own impending Passion, only serves to highlight the end of an old order that is based around the Judaism of the Old Testament, and the beginning of a new order that will have its fulfilment when Jesus returns. Together, these two chapters provide another major discourse in the Gospel of Matthew.

The teaching in Chapter 24 is initiated by a question from the disciples when they leave the impressive temple precincts. The reconstruction of the temple was undertaken by Herod the Great to curry favour with the Jews, and although Herod died many years before (4 BC), the temple—in all its architectural glory—is only now nearing completion. It is true to say that the noise of hammer and chisel would have been heard in the temple precincts throughout Jesus' ministry. His response to the disciples' comments about the temple is to give them some idea of the future: both the destiny of the temple and his own "*parousia*" or return. The most self-evident teaching in Matthew 24 is verses 34–35, which describe the circumstances and signs around the destruction of the temple, and likewise the final section (verses 36–51) is a description of the signs surrounding the *parousia*, Christ's Second Coming. The latter also, as it happens, answers the disciples' supplementary question after learning of the fate of the temple: ". . . what will be the sign of your coming and of the end of the age?" (24:3b). However, there are still some difficult interpretations to be considered, especially in relation to verses 29–31, but we shall come to these in due course.

What is clear in Jesus' response to the disciples' comments about the magnificence of the temple is that he knows the building's days are numbered (24:1–2). Its destiny is already decided; its shelf-life determined. The Roman legions under Vespasian, and then Titus, will eventually subjugate the initially successful Jewish revolt. And having suffered a number of reverses, the legions will successfully and brutally besiege Jerusalem. The revolt will be led by Eleazar ben Simon and the Zealots, although the leadership of the Jewish revolt from AD 64 will often be divided. In line with the rebellion of the Maccabees against Seleucid rule in 163 BC, the resistance—despite a year-long siege—will go down to the last man. Despite the pleas of the High Priest Ananias to save the temple and the city by parleying with the Romans, Eleazar ben Simon and his supporters were determined never to surrender to the Romans, and instead go down with the temple destroyed around their heads.[84] Thus it would come to pass. In the end (AD 70), the Romans would put the temple to the torch and destroy it, seemingly forever, with not one stone left on another. Jesus' shocking words, "I tell you the truth, not one stone here will be left on another; every one will be thrown down" (24:2), will be fulfilled. His prediction must shock the disciples profoundly, after all the years spent rebuilding the temple, and the sense of permanence that its new structure gave. Matthew, having presumably heard these words in person, is quite possibly recalling them now for his Jewish readers who, if the Gospel was written down after AD 70, already know the reality of these words of Jesus from the altered skyline of Jerusalem and the devastation of city and temple.

The temple was indeed rebuilt with a view to permanence, for its very large, surviving platform stones are still visible today in the Wailing Wall, but the words of Jesus have proved more lasting than the temple, as he said (24:35). No wonder the disciples go on to ask, "When will this [the destruction of the temple] happen?" (24:3b). In response, Jesus gives a series of indicators as to the timing of the disaster, and some pastoral advice as to *how* to approach those days.

Firstly, the period leading up to the destruction of the temple will be marked by instability and warfare. There will be many false messiahs.

In his *History of the Jewish War*, Josephus tells us of leaders who, if not messiahs in name, certainly came to liberate their people. There would be a period of terrible warfare: Josephus records over a million killed in the fighting and the final siege.[85] There are to be many people falsely claiming to be the Messiah. Indeed, R. T. France wrote that "there were plenty of such claimants in the unsettled years leading up to the Jewish revolt and the eventual destruction of the temple."[86] The whole period, but especially from the accession of Nero in AD 54, would be highly unstable, not becoming settled again until the accession of Vespasian at the end of the Julio-Claudian dynasty, stretching back to Augustus and Julius Caesar. So wars and rumours of wars, nation rising against nation, famines and earthquakes—not to mention the eruption of Vesuvius in AD 79—are all events that dominate this extraordinarily unstable period.

No wonder Jesus pauses to give his disciples advice and forewarning about the difficulties of these times. The Church, he says, will face persecution from its earliest days: "Then you will be handed over to be persecuted and put to death, and you will be hated by all nations because of me." (24:9). Nor does he stop there, but goes on to describe and predict the great stress of the years of the Jewish rebellion, culminating in the terrible siege of Jerusalem (24:15–25). When the standards of the Roman Legions are brought into the precincts of the temple, it will be an affront, says Jesus (24:15).[87] He rightly advises that in the days that are coming, people should not stay in the city where they will be put to the sword or be overwhelmed by famine, and where dead bodies will clog up the narrow streets, only to be consumed in the end by fire. Instead, counsels Jesus, get out of the city and flee to the hills, especially if you are pregnant. Don't delay on the rooftop, where you may have found temporary security, thinking you will be safe; don't be caught out by a Sabbath, when you can't travel for fear of breaking the Sabbath laws, with all their rigour, and find yourself trapped or find it difficult to buy food; don't wait until winter, when conditions are harsh. Instead, go just as soon as you can, and pass this information and advice on to your family, your children and your grandchildren, so that they will remember to take action. Lastly, says Jesus, don't be deceived that the Messiah will come and save you. He has already come, and when he returns it will be obvious to all, like a flash of lightning in the sky (24:27).

These days will be so difficult that the faith of many will be overwhelmed (24:10–13,22). Nevertheless, the Gospel will be preached to all nations as the early disciples scatter across the eastern Mediterranean. The Gospel will spread to Antioch, Cyprus, Asia and Europe (see Acts 8—20). The destruction of the temple will usher in the epoch of the Son of Man and his victory.

The next verses (24:29–31), beginning, "Immediately after the distress of those days . . .", can be read in one of two ways. The first is a very Jewish way, using apocalyptic language from Isaiah (see the quotation from Isaiah 13:10; 34:4). These verses refer to the two great events Jesus is predicting—the destruction of the temple and the *parousia*. At the same time, as was customary in Jewish Apocalyptic writing, Jesus collapses the period between them. Thus, in prophetic terms, or in a prophetic time frame, one event precipitates the other, even though there may be thousands of years between them, with the result that it is possible to speak of *both events* as following directly from each other, although this may overstretch credulity. The second way these verses may be read is that they indicate that Jesus really does think his return will take place during the first century AD, and that "immediately" (24:29) refers to the time soon after the destruction of the temple (see 24:36). Of the phrase, "But immediately after the distress of those days", R. T. France wrote that these words "constitute a formidable problem unless one is prepared to argue that Jesus (and Matthew) *really did expect* the *parousia* to take place in the late first century AD, and that Jesus was therefore mistaken."[88]

Nevertheless, even if the timing of the *parousia* is uncertain, and Jesus himself admits this, he can still answer their question, ". . . what will be the sign of your coming and of the end of the age?" (24:3b). To this Jesus now gives a comprehensive answer, despite saying he does not know exactly when it will be (24:36).

What are the signs of the *parousia*?

To the question, "When will the Second Coming or *parousia* happen?" the simple, yet vital answer is that no one knows, not even the Son of Man. Only the Father knows. If it is true that the Son of Man did not know, how much more true is it for us humans? However, the "predictions industry" is often feverish, and particularly around dates such as the millennium, when PMT (Pre-Millennial Tension) took on a whole new meaning. It is always the case when abnormal things happen in history (such as the Fall of Rome, the execution of King Charles I or the French Revolution), or when there are a number of severe natural catastrophes in swift succession, that events are read as signs that the return of Christ is imminent. But the simple truth, again, is that *no one knows* when it will happen, and even the Son of Man himself may have been mistaken; normal life will proceed normally (24:37–38), just as life proceeded normally before the sudden arrival of the flood in the days of Noah. The fact that Jesus describes how, during this time of crisis, one will be taken and the other left (24:40–41) is not a basis for a "Rapture" theory, in which the elect are suddenly removed to meet the Lord in the air, while the unregenerate are left behind, as depicted in films such as *A Thief in the Night* (1975), which featured Larry Norman's song "I Wish We'd All Been Ready". The film shows a husband being whisked off from his bathroom leaving an electric shaver running, a woman being taken from her kitchen with the tap running, and a child disappearing from a playground while others continue on the swings. The inference here is that the ones taken are saved and the ones left are condemned. There is nothing in the teaching of Jesus about where a person is taken or for what purpose. It could be for refuge and salvation, or it could be for judgement—we simply do not know. Nevertheless, to be ready (in the sense of living life in the anticipation of Christ's unexpected and sudden return) is both wise and obedient; and it is to this vital principle of readiness that Jesus now turns in helping his followers prepare for the *parousia* or Second Coming.

Preparing for the *parousia*

Much the greater part of the teaching in this section is about how to be ready. It is the implications of Christ's return, not the specific time, that should really concern us. In fact, the date is a distraction, but the discipline of our life is all-important. As C. S. Lewis said, when the author walks on to the stage, the play is over.[89] And the author of life, who created life and the universe in the first place, has every right to recreate it as he chooses, with an ending and a new beginning. Such a thought is firmly embedded in the Church's creeds and is an imperative in our discipleship. In a word, we should live in the light of his imminent return. Jesus gives a "pentateuch" of (five) parables to help us prepare for the *parousia*!

The first is about a neighbourhood watch, or household watch (24:42–44). In the unlikely circumstance of knowing that our house will be broken into, but not the precise time, we would take every precaution to prevent it happening: securing the doors and windows, keeping awake, being prepared. So Jesus, drawing his lesson from the parable, says, "[Y]ou also must be ready, because the Son of Man will come at an hour when you do not expect him."

The second of the short parables switches the focus from simply being ready, or alert, to discharging our responsibility in the time that is left to us: time either before our own demise or before the return of Jesus, whichever is sooner. As with many of the *parousia* parables, this has a master giving a charge to his servant before going away, but with the added factor that the master will return unexpectedly (24:45–51). Here the responsibility is that of a servant put in charge of the household, a kind of steward or house manager. The steward's task is to care for the other servants of this large establishment, which involves making sure they have the right food at the right time (24:45). Such a servant needs to be faithful and wise, and these are the qualities the master is looking for; the servant who fulfils the charge will be handsomely rewarded (24:46–47), but a lazy and irresponsible steward will be punished (24:48–51).

There is a natural correspondence between this parable and Christian ministry. Jesus appoints, in the household of his Church, servants who have the express responsibility of feeding his sheep.[90] Such servants have a duty to be faithful and wise in their care of the other members of the household. This care will involve pastoral oversight, sustained spiritual teaching and the careful administration of the Church, including the resolution of issues that arise. The point is that they must continue to do these things *until* the master returns, or until they no longer have that responsibility.

The parable concludes with a commendation and a sharp warning. The reward of the faithful and wise steward is that he or she will receive further responsibility, being put in charge of all the master's possessions (24:47). However, if the steward fails in his responsibility, abusing his fellow servants and getting drunk or self-indulgent, then he will be severely punished. The punishment described in the parable (being cut in two; 24:51) is shockingly harsh in order to demonstrate the seriousness of the failure and the importance of the responsibility, although such punishment was not unusual in the first century AD.

The text moves on to the third of the five parables, but employs a new and vivid metaphor: that of bridesmaids ("virgins" in most Bible translations) waiting for the arrival of the bridegroom (25:1–13). The figure of the bridegroom would become a standard description for Christ, not least in images from the Song of Songs, in Revelation 21, and in Paul's writing on marriage (see Song of Songs 2:16–3:11; Revelation 21:1–4; Ephesians 5:22–33). The metaphor Jesus uses here is of a group of bridesmaids waiting for the arrival of the bridegroom so that they might go with him and the bride to his house. A Jewish wedding at that time would be spread over several days, hence the danger of running out of wine (as at the wedding in Cana; John 2:3). The climax of the wedding was the feast at the home of the groom, where no doubt a religious ceremony took place before a rabbi or elder (later probably transferred to a synagogue). Exchanges of vows, rings, breaking a glass—possibly indicating that sorrow may accompany marriage—dancing and feasting are all part of the present-day Jewish marriage ceremony. A procession in which the bride was escorted to the bridegroom's home was still part of Jewish village weddings in nineteenth-century Russia. In Jesus' day this procession took place at night, with the bride riding a donkey or horse, taking a circuitous route back to the groom's home to show off the bride to all who would see.[91]

Furthermore, in Jesus' day the bridal party would wait with her bridesmaids to be escorted to the family home of her future husband, often in a torchlight procession. It is at this point in the parable that the bridegroom is delayed. The delay creates an issue of preparedness. So late is the bridegroom that the whole wedding party appears to have fallen asleep (25:5). Their lamps are perhaps left to burn on nearby ledges or tables, using up precious oil. When news comes that the bridegroom is near, the bridesmaids trim their lamps: that is, they prime the wicks by turning them up so they will burn brightly for the night procession. Then five who have not brought any spare oil find that their lamps are going out. The other five, the wise bridesmaids, have sufficient oil, but not enough to spare for the foolish ones who have none. While the foolish bridesmaids are shopping for oil from a night trader, the bridegroom arrives (25:10). They miss the procession and are shut out from the marriage feast. Even though they beat on the door, they are not let in. The lesson from the parable is clear: be ready, for we don't know the day or the hour when the Son of Man, the bridegroom of the Church, will return (25:13). To have "oil in our lamps to keep them burning" has been the song of the Church ever since. In practice, this means keeping the wick of faith alive in the power of the Spirit so that through prayer, waiting and good works, the disciple will be ready to welcome the returning bridegroom. Part of that alertness is rightly and profitably using the gifts or talents we have been given so that we are fruitful and the kingdom increases.

We turn next to the Parable of the Talents: the fourth of the *parousia* parables where this teaching is given. The Parable of the Talents (25:14–30), or in Luke, the Parable of the Pounds (Luke 19:11–27), is about stewardship of the treasure given by a master to his servants while he is away. In Luke, the parable has a more obvious historical setting, since it follows the actual history of Herod the Great and his son Archelaus, both of whom went to Rome to be appointed by Caesar as emperor–kings in Judea, in 40 BC and 4 BC respectively.[92] Although some of the details are different—talents in Matthew's account and "minas" or pounds in Luke's (approximately three months' salary), and in Luke's version the master going away to get a kingdom—the basic dynamic is the same: an absent lord who has entrusted gifts or money to his servants before a delayed or unexpected return ("After a long time," according to Matthew; 25:19).

This dynamic of leaving and returning provides the subjects with the opportunity for using the gifts given to them, in order to increase their value. In both parables, two of the servants manage to increase what they have been given to the extent of doubling their value (25:19–23), but one servant fails to make any increase at all (25:24–25). Two are praised and one is severely judged for failing to do anything with what he has been given. Indeed, this failure appears to be fuelled by a misunderstanding of his lord. From fear of failing he attempts nothing, thinking his master will be angry if he loses everything in the endeavour. Yet to attempt nothing is worse than trying and failing, we are told. He tries nothing and gains nothing, so now he receives worse than nothing (25:26–28), for "even what he has" is taken away and given to the others. The closing lesson is that "everyone who has will be given more, and they will have an abundance. Whoever does not have, even what they have will be taken from them" (25:29).

Discipleship is therefore about using the gifts and opportunities we have been given. Identifying those gifts, and their consequent ministries, is the task of the individual set in the community of the Church, which in turn has ways of establishing these gifts, and providing scope for their use. There will be opportunities to speak or pray or serve, or to begin a new endeavour. The provision of those opportunities is the task of leadership; the taking of those opportunities is like investing and developing the talents in the parable. I have seen a host of ministries develop within the local church: care for—and discipleship of—differently-abled people and children; provision of spiritual and social support for young people on the margins of society; care for those in hospital through visiting and chapel services; providing pastors to oversee our city streets on busy weekend nights; feeding and sheltering those who have no food or nowhere to stay; teaching and leading the many discipleship groups of the church, from parents with infants to the most senior citizen in her nineties. All these variegated ministries provide opportunities for the increase of gifts. Furthermore, there is a natural connection between the increase of these talents and the care of the needy in Matthew's final *parousia* parable, about preparation for Christ's return.

During a recent visit to Rome, which was a gift from our last parish on retirement, we naturally went to the Vatican Museum, that treasure trove of art and decoration over the centuries. Along with thousands of others (twenty-three thousand in a day, we were told!), we gazed up in wonder at Michelangelo's painting of the Sistine Chapel ceiling, and in particular, at the famous rendering of the creation of Adam. Yet I was personally drawn to a picture in the medieval section of the Art Gallery which could not have been simpler or more compelling; it was depicted "six ministries to the poor". The thinking behind the painting is found in Matthew's Parable of the Sheep and the Goats, where the separation of sheep and goats is based on the response to six needy groups: the hungry, the thirsty, refugees, the naked, the sick and the imprisoned. Perhaps we should all intentionally seek to alleviate one or more of these needs, whether locally in our communities, or internationally. This could be done either in partnership with an organization or through direct contact with one or more of these needy groups in our neighbourhoods. The leadership of our local church in Hungerford, which is in a prosperous part of the world, tell us each week the number of families who have no food and have accessed a food bank, and what food is needed.

The Parable of the Sheep and the Goats (25:31–46) is surely one of the best-known parables of Jesus, along with the Prodigal Son, the Good Samaritan, and the Sower. There is a solemnity, a power and an inexorable rhythm of justice to the parable that is very telling. The Son of Man's majesty is untrammelled: he is surrounded by angels, seated on the throne in heavenly glory, with all nations gathered before him. It is awesome. The judgement proceeds with a farming metaphor. Flocks in Palestine were often made up of sheep and goats pasturing together, as I have also seen in Greece. There comes a time, however, when they must be separated. In the parable, the sheep are the righteous and are set on the king's right hand. The goats, however, are the unfaithful ones, set on the left hand of the master. The grounds for their separation are given next: the sheep, or righteous ones, have responded with compassion to the needs of the six suffering groups, and are thus saved, while those represented by the goats have not. "But when have we seen you hungry, thirsty, naked, a refugee, sick, or imprisoned?" ask the sheep. When they alleviated the needs of their fellow humans (their "neighbours"—see Luke 10:25–37), comes the answer. The sentence at the heart of the parable is, "Whatever you did for one of the least of these brothers or sisters of mine, you did for me." (25:40). Likewise, whatever the goats, or unrighteous, did *not do* for the needy they *did not do* for the master.

At the root of this parable is Jesus' complete identification with the poor. This is a theme picked up by Leo Tolstoy in his short story "Where Love Is, God Is" (1885). A poor cobbler, Martin, who has lost his wife and all his children, is promised in a dream that he will meet Christ. The next day he cares for three people: an impoverished and frozen street-sweeper, a desperate mother with her infant child, and an urchin who has stolen an apple from a *babushka*. He feels cheated, initially, that he never met Christ; only in a subsequent dream is he told that in caring for those who were in need he has truly met his Lord. How we treat such needy people is how we treat Jesus, and treating them with compassionate action is the truest sign of sure faith in Christ, the master. Failure to treat the poor with compassionate care questions the validity of faith, and opens the way for our own rejection by God, with all that that means (25:41,46). Preparation for the *parousia*, therefore, means care for the poor. One Victorian social reformer, Lord Shaftesbury (1801–1885), kept the *parousia* at the centre of his thoughts. This drove him to reform the Factory Acts, among other things, thereby limiting the exploitation of children in mills, mines or as chimney sweeps.

In this way, and with these parables, Jesus prepares the disciples for his return. No one, not even Jesus himself—who may even have thought his return was imminent in the first century AD—knows when it will be (24:36). It will follow the destruction of the temple, however, and there will be times of severe testing ahead. All disciples are to be alert, faithfully discharging their ministry tasks, sustained in their waiting by the oil of the Spirit, using and developing their gifts, and loving the poor as they alleviate their needs. In these ways, the followers of Jesus will be prepared for his *parousia* in their lifetime or after their own departure, whichever comes first. The kingdom is surely coming, and for this eventuality they are also preparing. Notice of the advent of the kingdom is given through the death and resurrection of Jesus, to which we finally turn in Chapter 13.

CHAPTER 13

Fulfilment of God's Plan

Matthew 20:17–28:20

We come now to the culmination of Jesus' ministry on earth, the final eight chapters of the Gospel. Approximately a quarter of Matthew's Gospel is spent on this final week of ministry. Within these chapters, as we have seen, Jesus both castigates the spirituality of the Pharisees (Matthew 23) and teaches about his return and the days leading up to the destruction of the temple (Matthew 24 and 25). Around the time of this teaching we have the entry of Jesus into Jerusalem, on what we now call Palm Sunday; his answers to many questions designed to trip him up; parables told to show the inclusion of the Gentiles (an important point for Matthew, explaining to the Jewish church that the Gentiles are included in God's plan); the narrative leading up to the crucifixion; the crucifixion itself; the climactic event of the resurrection; and the mission of Christ to the world. In all, there are seven distinct episodes which we will look at in turn.

The entry into Jerusalem

That Jesus chooses to ride into Jerusalem on a donkey is both a fulfilment of Old Testament prophecy of a king entering the city in the same way, and a symbolic act denoting the style of his kingship. Normally Jesus walks everywhere and there is no other account of him riding a donkey. Now, through a prearranged plan, Jesus is seated on a donkey as he enters Jerusalem (21:1–3). Riding into the city is a deliberate act of symbolism and fulfilment. Matthew is quick to tell us that what Jesus does is a fulfilment of the prophecy of Zechariah: "See, your king comes to you, gentle and riding on a donkey, on a colt, the foal of donkey" (21:5, cf. Zechariah 9:9). There is a seeming contradiction here. Kings generally ride chargers or travel in chariots; certainly this was true of Assyrian and Egyptian kings, but Jesus—a different sort of king—comes on a donkey. He is therefore the humble Messiah or the lowly king, but for all that, he is still acclaimed by the people. A very large crowd (*"pleistos ochlos"*— meaning "as large a crowd as you can think of"; 21:8) has assembled and they spontaneously break into praise. They accompany Jesus down the Mount of Olives, shouting acclamations and laying branches in his path as a mark of honour and acclaim.

The cries of "Hosanna to the Son of David!" and "Blessed is he who comes in the name of the Lord!" (21:9) come from the last and longest of the *"Hallel"* or praise psalms (Psalms 113–118), traditionally sung at the major festivals in Jerusalem. *"Hosanna"* is a Greek form of the Hebrew words translated "save us!" in Psalm 118,[93] a cry for God's rescue leading to his blessing, and addressed to Jesus as the Son of David, a messianic and kingly figure. When Jesus enters Jerusalem, the whole city is stirred.

Jerusalem has not had the same exposure to Jesus as the Galilee crowd, so they ask, "Who is this?" (21:10). The enthusiastic response comes back, "This is Jesus, the prophet from Nazareth in Galilee" (21:11), although he is originally from Bethlehem, in fact, and hence the Son of David (1:17; 2:5–6). Clearly even the Galileans are not yet fully aware of his true identity. Nevertheless, "[t]he people of the city have every reason to see trouble ahead as the unruly Galilean crowd bring 'their' prophet into Jerusalem in a royal procession."[94] The trouble comes more quickly than they could ever have imagined.

Jesus probably goes directly to the temple, now more or less complete since its refurbishment under Herod the Great. It is here in the Court of the Gentiles that a unofficial market has been set up by traders. Money is changed into the Tyrian temple coinage, no doubt generating a handy profit for the temple authorities. It is here that sacrificial animals are bought, pigeons for the poor and lambs for the better-off. It is here that the male population pays the temple tax, in the temple currency, which Jesus has reluctantly paid for himself and Peter by catching a fish that has the tax money in its mouth (17:24–27). It is this sight of incessant trade and money-making that confronts Jesus on his entrance to the temple precincts. It infuriates him to see the "house of prayer for all nations" (see Isaiah 56:6–8) being used in this way, exploiting Jewish pilgrims for cash and foreigners for income. [95] "You're making the temple a 'den of robbers'," he says (21:13; cf. Jeremiah 7:11), and he overturns the tables of the traders in his anger. Still, amidst the commotion he heals the lame and reproves the Jewish leaders. Children continue to sing their refrain of praise, even in the temple precincts as this goes on, an echo of the earlier praise on the way down the Mount of Olives, and this incenses the religious leaders. Children may be seen, but not heard, especially not heard giving praise to Jesus. The Jewish leaders are offended and ask him to silence the ebullient children. Jesus is ready with a riposte from the Psalms: "From the lips of children and infants you have ordained praise" (21:16; Psalm 8:2). He then leaves the city to spend the night at Bethany.

Any questions?

The next week is characterized in part by Jesus being asked a host of questions, mostly with a hidden (or not so hidden) catch to them, so that he might be accused by the authorities of misleading the people. There are five questions in all. The first is posed the day after his overthrowing of the tables of the money changers and stallholders in the Court of the Gentiles and at the start of his teaching in the temple. It is a genuine question about authorization and comes from the Jewish leaders: "By what authority are you doing these things?" (that is, overthrowing the traders' tables in the temple and teaching in the temple courts; 21:23).

Jesus responds reluctantly to the question, unwilling to declare who he is. Such a direct declaration of his divinity, and the claim that he is authorized by his Father or YAHWEH, is never Jesus' preferred way of identifying himself. He prefers to speak of himself in the third person, most frequently calling himself the Son of Man. And on many occasions Jesus has strictly cautioned the disciples and those he has healed not to say that he is the Messiah (see 9:30; 16:20; 17:9). In other words, he prefers people to come to their own conclusions. So he does not answer directly here (21:24–27). Instead, as so often, he answers one question with another: "John's baptism," he asks, "where did it come from? Was it from heaven, or from human beings?" The leaders ponder their answer. If they say, "From heaven," then why did they not believe John? If they say, "From human beings," they are in danger of losing the respect of the people, since John is highly regarded. So they keep silent, saying they don't know. Because they give no answer, out of expediency, rather than declaring their real convictions, Jesus feels justified in not declaring the truth of his identity, which they would either only decry or use as the basis of a charge against him. He too remains silent about his full identity and authority.

The second question, posed after a number of parables, is found in Matthew 22:15–22. This is the famous question about whether or not it is right to pay taxes to Caesar, and in particular the poll tax levied by the Romans since AD 6. It is a well-crafted question, judged to bring maximum embarrassment to Jesus. If he says the Jews *should* pay taxes, he will be marked out as a collaborator with a pagan power; if he says the Jews should *not* pay the tax, he could be deemed a rebel and a dangerous insurgent or rabble-rouser against Rome. Either way the Pharisees, having carefully concocted the question, feel sure Jesus will be damned. Instead, Jesus memorably asks for a coin (which he does not have on him) and in a remarkable one-liner says, "Give to Caesar what is Caesar's, and to God what is God's" (22:21). This answer begs a further question about what is legitimately Caesar's and what is rightfully God's, but it silences the Pharisees and demonstrates Jesus' profound wisdom. The Pharisees go away to lick their intellectual and spiritual wounds. They will come back one more time, but now it is the turn of their rivals, the Sadducees.

The Sadducees come with what is a ridiculous-sounding question, driven by their conviction that there is no resurrection (22:23–32). They concoct an absurd story designed to show the difficulty of belief in the resurrection. They hope to demean the possibility of life after death by an argument that is a *reductio ad absurdum*. In their story, seven brothers fulfil their levirate duty by each in turn marrying a widow, after the unlikely event of the successive deaths of all the brothers who had been her husband (22:24–28).[96] In the resurrection life, they wonder, whose wife will she be? Jesus' answer revolves around two things: the Scriptures and the power of God. The Scriptures teach that God is the God of the living, for he is the God of Abraham, Isaac and Jacob, who are alive to him, so therefore, in principle, there must be a resurrection, otherwise God would be the God of the dead. More than that, the power of God can enable the resurrection to take place, as will be supremely demonstrated with Jesus. Furthermore, in heaven there will be no marriage. Men and women will be like angels (22:30), capable of deep love, but no longer in exclusive or sexual relationships. Procreation will no longer be needed. In other words, marriage and procreation are temporary earthly arrangements. The Early Church Fathers—especially Augustine and the Cappadocian Fathers—made much of this. Far from diminishing the reality of the resurrection, Jesus elucidates it further.

Having heard that Jesus has effectively "silenced" the Sadducees, the Pharisees ask their final question (22:36). This one has no particular political edge to it. It is essentially about the law and its most important commandments. Although Jesus' summary of the law is familiar to us, his combination of the teaching in Deuteronomy 6:5 and Leviticus 19:18 is, in fact, both original and liberating. For out of the hundreds of Old Testament laws—the twelfth-century Jewish scholar Maimonides from Cordoba calculated that there were six hundred and thirteen commands in the Torah—Jesus summarizes the most important priorities for human life (22:37–40). The first is to love God, now revealed in Jesus Christ, with our whole selves, the second to love our neighbour even as we love ourselves. These two commandments provide the supreme guide to the object of our loving and the greatest obligation upon our lives. At the same time as being all-encompassing, and involving all aspects of our human life (heart, soul and mind), this summary of the law is also liberating,in the sense that there is nothing more that is required. To love as Jesus suggests is to fulfil the law. There is no need to look elsewhere for further instruction or for other commandments. Love is therefore the fulfilling of the law: loving God, loving neighbour, and loving self. Holding this loving together is the calling of every disciple.

The fifth question is addressed *by* Jesus *to* the Pharisees. In response to their probing, he has a question about the Messiah. Whose son is he (22:41–42)? They reply, correctly, that he is the Son of David. True though this is, Jesus thinks their interpretation of the title is inadequate. For the Messiah is more than simply the descendant of David, and to bear this out he quotes the Psalmist (22:43–44; Psalm 110:1), where David prophesies, "The Lord [YAHWEH] said to my Lord [the Son of David or Son of Man]: 'Sit at my right hand until I put your enemies under your feet.'" Jesus then asks how it is that God or YAHWEH addresses the Messiah as "my Lord" (i.e., David's Lord) in this way, if he is just David's son. The answer, surely, is that although he is a descendant of David, he is also David's Lord, and one whom the Father says will sit at his right hand with all his enemies subject to him. Since the Pharisees know that Jesus is claiming to be the Messiah, this is not simply a claim to being a descendant of David, but a claim to supreme authority given by YAHWEH himself. This may sound like a peculiarly Jewish argument to us, but for Matthew's Jewish readers it was another statement of the authority of Jesus and his fulfilment of messianic prophecy in the Old Testament.

The Pharisees have no more questions. Indeed, no one dares ask him anything else, especially questions of the kind designed to trip him up (22:46). Anyone in our postmodern society claiming faith in God is liable to be asked difficult questions. The underlying question of many will be how we can hold to a Christian explanation of life with so many conflicting opinions in the world. It is worth, therefore, giving thought to some of the most frequently asked questions. Not that we might have "pat" answers, but so that we might show we have given careful thought to common questions, even if in many instances there are few simple answers.

Jesus not only gives profound answers that often require further thought, but between his answers he also tells his audience a number of highly provocative parables about the future of the Jewish nation and the mission of God.

The provocative parables

There are four of these parables, all expressing the same disturbing theme. One of them is what is generally called an "enacted parable": the cursing of the fig tree, which occurs when Jesus re-enters the city following the clearance of the money changers and traders from the temple, having spent a night in Bethany (21:17–22). The others are the Parable of the

Two Sons, the Parable of the Tenants and the Parable of the Wedding Banquet. The three spoken parables elucidate the enacted parable: Israel at the time—like the fig tree—is barren, incapable of producing fruit, and will be cursed or judged. It is for this reason too (what some call the "supersession of Israel", meaning the incorporation of faithful Israel into the new community of the Church) that Jesus goes on to explain the destruction of the temple, which will no longer be needed (24:1-35).[97] Concerning the objection that the fig tree is not in its fruit-bearing season and so can hardly be expected to produce figs, the answer must be that Israel is indeed in season; her long-awaited Messiah is present with her, but is ignored or condemned—and so there is no fruit. A fig tree with foliage might have the promise of one fig, a sign of an approaching harvest, but this fig tree has none at all. As Micah said,

> What misery is mine!
> I am like one who gathers summer fruit
>   at the gleaning of the vineyard;
> there is no cluster of grapes to eat,
>   none of the early figs that I crave.
> The faithful have been swept from the land;
>   not one upright person remains.
> Everyone lies in wait to shed blood;
>   they hunt each other with nets.
>
> *Micah 7:1-2*

These words of imminent bloodshed are about to be fulfilled, and Israel is not about to produce the long-awaited fruit.

The remaining three parables, which are told back to back (21:28—22:14), together with Jesus' "woes" over the Pharisees (chapter 23) and his prophecy about the destruction of the temple, make for very sobering and bleak reading. The three parables, although each has a different setting, share a similar message. What is entrusted to a privileged group will be taken away and given to others. In the case of the two sons (21:28-32), only the repentant older son will gain, because he is obedient to his father, doing what is required (despite initial disobedience). Jesus draws out the implications of this: the tax collectors and prostitutes are entering the kingdom ahead of the Jewish leaders, because they believe the teaching of John the Baptist whereas the Jewish establishment does not. Similarly, but more pointedly, in their parable (21:33–44), the tenants are given the privilege of a fine vineyard, but when their produce is requested by the landlord, they kill his servants and, ultimately, even his son. Jesus draws out the implication with great clarity and foreboding: "I tell you that the kingdom of God will be taken away from you and given to a people who will produce its fruit" (21:43).

The final Parable of the Wedding Banquet is well known. Those invited refuse to come, so caught up are they in their business. They "pay no attention", and even kill the king's messengers (22:5–6). Others are invited to the banquet, which must be filled, and those who have failed to come or who have come wrongly dressed—either refusing the proffered wedding garment (Augustine's explanation) or attired in dress or conduct unbecoming—are punished.

In each case, those privileged with a filial relationship, such as the second son, or with a fine vineyard, or a great invitation, fail to produce the fruit or response expected. In each case, what they have is taken away from them, and furthermore they suffer judgement. Such pointed parables can have only one meaning: the Jewish nation has ample opportunity to produce the fruit expected of it, but fails. This failure will provide the opportunity for others, notably the Gentiles and "sinners", to enter in where they have stumbled. If we bear in mind that Matthew's audience was initially mostly Jewish, here is a frank explanation by Jesus of God's economy: what has been given will be taken away so that what has not yet been experienced can be enjoyed by others, with the effect of making the Jews think again in the future.[98] All of this is the necessary background to the rapidly advancing events of the Passion. These events will be prepared for by conspiracy, by anointing, by betrayal, by a meal and by prayer.

Preparation for the Passion

Even as Jesus is finishing his teaching about the future in response to the question from the disciples about when his *parousia* will be (24:3), the leaders of the Jewish nation are plotting his end (26:1–5). The High Priest, Caiaphas, together with the leaders of the people, decides that Jesus must be arrested with a view to his execution, but not in front of the festival crowd, as such an action might backfire (26:5).

Meanwhile, Jesus stays in Bethany, just outside Jerusalem, where he is anointed with expensive perfume. Luke tells a similar story earlier in his Gospel of a prostitute anointing Jesus while he is dining at the house of another Simon, a Pharisee, who lives in Galilee (Luke 7:36–50). Matthew's story in Bethany is remarkably similar to the anointing of Jesus by Mary, the spiritually-minded sister of Lazarus, told in John's Gospel (John 12:1–11), but Matthew's account of Jesus being anointed is set in the house of Simon the Leper (26:6–13). Both John's and Matthew's accounts have a very similar conversation revolving around the extravagance of the action; the waste of expensive perfume that could have been sold, with the proceeds given to the poor; the fact that the act is a preparation for Jesus' burial; and the way this action will later become known around the world. Either Matthew confuses the anointing at Simon's house with the anointing by Mary at her home, or there are three anointings: two which take place in Bethany, with remarkably similar conversations, and one which takes place earlier, in another Simon's house in Galilee (Luke 7:36–50). Whatever the actual details of the story, what is inescapable is the devotion of each woman's faith, the beauty of her actions, the fragrance of the perfume filling the house, and the dignity which these actions bestow on Jesus. It is truly an act of worship, which is celebrated wherever it is recalled. What could be in greater contrast to this woman's exorbitant, extravagant worship of Jesus than the greed of Judas, who—in the very next verses—agrees to betray his teacher with thirty pieces of silver (26:14–16)? The one gives, the other grasps: the one is full of love in her giving: the other is soon full of remorse for his taking.

The preparation of Jesus now moves on to two profound events: the Last Supper (26:17–30), and the Agony in Gethsemane (26:36–46). It was the custom for Jews to eat the Passover meal on the eve of the feast, which in the Jewish calendar is Nisan 14.[99] The Passover meal is a commemorative meal and a perpetual ordinance (see Exodus 12:1–27), recalling the deliverance of Israel, when the Angel of Death passed over the Israelite houses protected by the blood of the Passover Lamb daubed on their lintels. Every year their deliverance is remembered. Households gather together, and the story is retold in the context of the ritualized meal of Passover.

Having found the upper room, the use of which Jesus has prearranged, the disciples settle down to eat the meal, but it is to be no ordinary Passover supper. First, Jesus sends feelings of dread around the room when he says someone will betray him. Later Judas is identified as the betrayer (26:25b), and he swiftly leaves (though only John actually states this). The normal symbolism of the meal is further changed. Jesus takes bread, and his doing so is related with four critical verbs: he *took* the bread, he *gave* thanks, he *broke* it, and he *gave* it. His words—"Take and eat; this is my body"—are of great significance, with the bread representing his body (26:26). For though his body is then with them at the table, it is about to be broken on the cross and will go on to nourish the disciples as spiritual food. Next Jesus takes the cup and makes a profoundly shocking statement: "Drink from it, all of you. This is my blood of the covenant [some manuscripts have '*new* covenant'], which is poured out for many for the forgiveness of sins" (26: 27–28). Although the full significance could not have dawned on the disciples until some time later, his blood—shed on the cross and memorialized in this meal—is to become the blood of the covenant that replaces the sacrifices of the Old Testament with one single sacrifice for the forgiveness of sins. It will ratify a new covenant, the true and lasting covenant of grace between God and humankind. That the disciples must drink and eat not only makes this sign personal and individual as well as communal, it also provides an occasion for a spiritual feeding on the reality of Christ's death. In trying to explain the process of this means of grace, Christians, as with other mysteries such as the incarnation and the Trinity, sometimes lose the spiritual reality by over-constructing a rational or philosophical explanation, not content to leave it as an unfathomable mystery. Jesus offers a way of remembering him and his death that will sustain his people on their journey. He will wait to drink the wine until he feasts with his people in his Father's kingdom (26:29).

The final work of preparation, for Jesus especially, is the prayer in the Garden of Gethsemane. There are few more profound moments in the Bible or in the story of our salvation than these minutes of excruciating prayer. The garden, which lies at the foot of the Mount of Olives and is still there today with its ancient olive trees—continuing to bear witness to Jesus' agony—was a favourite resort of Jesus. This is a final moment of privacy before the events of his Passion take their predicted shape, and the course of redemption, planned before the world began (1 Peter 1:20), is disclosed. For Jesus, it is the last moment of uninterrupted prayer to his Father about his forthcoming suffering and sacrifice. Here Jesus, in the days of his flesh, is wrestling with the projected plan of offering himself as a sacrifice for human sin (see Hebrews 5:7–10).

Having arrived in the Garden, Jesus takes the three inner-circle disciples, Peter, James, and John, a little further with him. He encourages them to prepare by prayer as well. He then goes a little distance from them to pray. The gist of his prayer is to ask if there is any other way besides the way of the cross (which Jesus knows awaits him) that he might take. While searching his own and the Father's heart for a different way, he nevertheless submits himself to the will of the Father, which he voluntarily accepts (26:39). If we interpose at this point the reality of the Trinity and the truth that Jesus and the Father are one (John 14:9 and 17:20–21), then this agonized exploration in prayer becomes a final searching of God's will and not the unwilling railing of a son against suffering forced on him by an unfeeling Father (John 10:18). When the well-known atheist Richard Dawkins asks if there is not another way whereby God could bring salvation to humanity apart from the sacrifice of Jesus, he has neither understood the righteousness of God, nor the extent of human guilt, nor the extraordinary free forgiveness about to be secured through this voluntarily embraced solution. Justice and mercy do combine perfectly, if unfathomably, in the wisdom of the cross. Asking three times that his cup of suffering, both physical and spiritual, might be removed, is a prayerful exploration conducted with natural human shrinking from the physical and spiritual pain which lies ahead, but also a struggle that displays both the humanity and the divinity of Jesus in their momentarily conflicted integrity. Because of the intensity, Luke tells us that Jesus' sweat turns into great drops of blood on this chill spring evening, a further sign of the profound internal struggle Jesus suffers in anticipation of his passion. In the end an angel strengthens him (Luke 22:43–44). When Jesus rises from prayer after his third intercession, he is *prepared* in a way that the sleeping disciples are not. They cannot watch with him. They do not appreciate the intense trial they too will face, and will mostly fail. They do not realize that "[t]he spirit is willing, but the body is weak" (26:41b). They sleep when they might have prayed. Their sleep leaves them *unprepared*.

A band of temple soldiers or guards arrives through the olive trees, led by Judas (26:47), and nothing can now prevent the Son of Man being delivered up into the hands of sinful men.

The trials of Jesus

The arrest of Jesus serves to show the unpreparedness of the disciples. They seek to prevent what Jesus knows must take place. Judas, with utter hypocrisy and insouciance, identifies Jesus to the guard with a kiss. He thus betrays Jesus into the hands of his enemies. Amazingly, Jesus addresses Judas as "friend" (26:50). While Jesus accepts the course of events, indeed shows some determination that Judas get on with it (26:50), the disciples seek to resist the arrest. Peter pulls out a sword and slices off the ear of Malchus (the servant of the High Priest). And then Jesus, with what is one of his most important sayings—"[A]ll who draw the sword will die by the sword" (26:52)—restores the ear. If force is required, Jesus can draw on unassailable power (twelve legions of angels), but then the Scriptures would not be fulfilled, nor would salvation be secured. It is not a question of force, but of power directed by wisdom. Tragically, the Church has too frequently allied its mission to the sword, taking its pursuit of orthodoxy to the fires of heresy or the torture of the rack, leaving a trail of blood across 1,900 years of human history, where other ways should have triumphed, ways which were exemplified on this day.

Jesus reproves the temple guards and their leaders for this surreptitious arrest, at night and in secret, but then acknowledges that their very cowardliness is a fulfilment of the prophets' words (26:55–56). The Passion narrative in Matthew moves on to include two trials (before the Sanhedrin and before Pilate), and acts of deep regret by two disciples for their denial and betrayal respectively.

The first trial is before the Jewish Sanhedrin, the Council of seventy leaders of Israel, consisting of Sadducees and Pharisees who governed Jewish affairs from Jerusalem. One member was Nicodemus (John 3:1). The trial consists of two parts: an earlier hearing at night after the arrest of Jesus, then an early morning judgement, since the court is not supposed to hear capital trials after dark, according to the Mishnah. The evidence against Jesus is brought by two witnesses, in line with Jewish law: no one could be condemned without the evidence of two witnesses (see Numbers 35:30; Deuteronomy 17:6; 19:15). The evidence given is that Jesus has been heard to say he will destroy the temple and rebuild it in three days. Jesus may have said this (see John 2:19), but it was never literally meant. Jesus keeps silent when accused, but when asked by the High Priest whether he is "the Christ, the Son of God", he assents saying, "In future you will see the Son of Man sitting at the right hand of the Mighty One and coming on the clouds of heaven" (26:64). Citing Daniel (7:13), Jesus uses his preferred title of the Son of Man, and makes the solemn declaration that he is the Messiah who will be seated at the right hand of the Mighty One. Such a claim is blasphemy if untrue. The High Priest, who has long ago discounted Jesus as the Messiah, rends his clothes and calls for the death penalty. At that point the physical as well as the verbal abuse of Jesus begins (26:67–68).

Before the second trial in front of Pilate the following morning, two of Jesus' disciples are overwhelmed by regret and remorse: Peter for his denial and Judas for his betrayal. Despite his earlier protestation of undying loyalty when Jesus predicted his denial (26:31–35), Peter—unprepared— is overcome by fear when challenged (26:69–75). Peter denies his Lord three times, in spite of Jesus' forewarning that he will do so and advice in Gethsemane that Peter should pray for strength (26:40–41). Peter reckons on his *own* strength, which comes crashing down around him when confronted by the simple challenges of serving maids (26:69,71). Fear replaces bravado and self-preservation overwhelms loyalty. Only when faced with such a choice is the true nature of Peter's fragility revealed. When the cock crows, the awful realization dawns on him that he is far weaker than he had estimated himself to be, and he is appalled that his loyalty to Jesus should dissolve so quickly. With the cock crowing he remembers Jesus' words to him, and goes out and weeps bitterly (26:75).

Judas, by contrast, is overwhelmed by a terrible darkness. Over time he has allowed himself to be overtaken by greed. John tells us that Judas, driven by greed, has become a thief (John 12:6). In fact, in becoming the treasurer for the corporate life of the disciples he has put himself in the way of temptation, into which he has habitually fallen. Thieving has become a habit, so the chance of betraying Jesus to the authorities for thirty pieces of silver becomes irresistible. Yet as the Passion of Jesus progresses and his death seems inevitable after his condemnation by the Sanhedrin (27:1–2), the realization dawns in Judas' heart of the depths to which he has sunk. Matthew tells us he is seized with remorse, not repentance, and is held by dark despair and deep guilt, aware of his sin (27:4). He tries to return the betrayal money to ease his conscience, but he cannot turn back the clock. Unable to live with the guilt and shame, or to live with himself or with those he has come to know through Jesus, he decides on suicide. He believes he has no hope of forgiveness, so no cause for repentance. We cannot be sure of his eternal destiny; at the time he is hope-less and doesn't want to live any longer. Those who hire him, the Chief Priests and the elders, have no concern for him, so with the religious fastidiousness to which they are prone, they are willing to engineer Jesus' death, but are scrupulous about handling the money they have used to set his judicial murder in train. Such is the casuistry and rationalization of evil: they fulfil Jesus' words of a few days earlier—"You strain out a gnat but swallow a camel" (23:24). This is the largest camel of all.

The second part of the two-part trial by the High Priests and elders of the people concludes in the morning following Jesus' arrest (27:1–2), and he is sentenced to death. However, for the enforcement of their decision Pilate, the Roman governor, must still try Jesus. He is led away to the Governor's palace, to appear before Pilate. As in all the Gospels, the substance of Pilate's trial of Jesus is the reported claim that he takes the title "the king of the Jews". Pilate therefore asks Jesus whether he has ever made such a claim: "Are you the king of the Jews?" (27:11). Jesus assents to the title in an indirect way, replying, "Yes, it is as you say," but thereafter—to Pilate's consternation—he remains silent (27:14). Pilate, convinced of his innocence, seeks to release Jesus, finding no basis in the charges against him. He tries for a prisoner exchange: releasing Jesus and instead executing Barabbas, a notorious rebel. But the crowd shouts for Barabbas's release and the crucifixion of Jesus. Pilate's wife has a disturbing dream and advises that Jesus should be released forthwith (27:19). Still the crowd cries for his crucifixion. In a vain attempt to shift the guilt from himself, Pilate asks for water and symbolically washes his hands of the decision he is about to take (27:24). Thereupon he hands Jesus over to the soldiers for crucifixion.

The Passion of Jesus

Given its gravity and its place in our salvation, the account of the crucifixion of Jesus in Matthew's Gospel is remarkably short, barely a single chapter. The preliminaries to the execution on the cross are much longer than the account of the crucifixion itself. Each Gospel writer alights on different aspects: Mark and Matthew are very similar; Luke includes the conversation with the penitent thief (Luke 23:39–43); John focuses on the kingship of Jesus and the inscription above the cross, the word to his mother, and his physical death (John 19:19–22,25–27,31–37).

Matthew recounts the flogging and mocking of Jesus by the platoon of soldiers about to execute him, and the forcing of Simon to carry Jesus' cross (27:27–32), as well as his moment of crucifixion (27:34–35). The description is detailed, but brief: Jesus is offered drugged wine to drink, which he refuses; the soldiers gamble for his meagre possessions; the charge is fixed to the cross; the robbers are crucified alongside Jesus; and a helpless, totally vulnerable Jesus is mocked (27:39–44).

There is a change of tone between the sixth and the ninth hours (12 noon to 3 p.m.). It is as though these three hours take us to the heart of Jesus' work on the cross. What the Gospel describes briefly, the Epistles will go on to explain at greater length. Matthew tells us that in these hours

Jesus feels himself abandoned by his Father, expressing this abandonment in the great cry of dereliction: "My God, my God, why have you forsaken me?" (27:46). The Epistles will tell us he is bearing the guilt of sin in his own body on the tree (for example, Romans 3:25; Ephesians 1:7; Colossians 2:14; 1 Peter 2:24; Hebrews 9:11–14). During these hours he bears the guilt of humankind; the dark cloud on his soul which feels as if the Father has abandoned him leads to this agonised cry. At the same time, God the Father is mysteriously in Christ, reconciling the world to himself (2 Corinthians 5:19). With this truth in mind, there can be no crude suggestion that the Father is angry with the Son on our account. Equally, the death of Jesus in a very real way turns away the wrath and deep disappointment of God against and with the human race.

> The New Testament authors never attribute the atonement either to Christ in such a way as to disassociate him from the Father, or to God in such a way as to dispense with Christ, but rather to God and Christ . . .[100]

The mystery is that God is always *in Christ* as he reconciles the world to himself, while Jesus, fully God and man whilst suffering on the cross, feels himself abandoned by the Father. What we know is that Jesus is dying our death, on our behalf, that we might live his life. Or as Athanasius puts it, "He became as we are that we might become as he is."[101]

The sign that Jesus has finished his redemptive work on the cross, and that this is the concluding event of Matthew's Passion narrative, is the splitting of the temple curtain (27:51). When Jesus gives up his spirit, the temple curtain separating the Holy of Holies from the Court of the Jews is torn in two: the way to the Father is open, made possible by the Son, and enabled by the Spirit. The cross has indeed "done it all". The bystanders are awestruck: the centurion confesses Jesus to be the Son of God. The women watch the last moments of Christ's life ebbing away, wrapped in concentrated grief. Supernatural events occur through the city (27:51–56).

Joseph of Arimathea (a Judean town some twenty miles north-west of Jerusalem) is a follower of Jesus. At some point, this wealthy man has come to believe Jesus to be the Messiah; now he determines to care for his body and to give it a decent burial (27:57–60). With the help of Nicodemus (see John 19:39), and maybe some household servants, they take the body down from the cross, having permission from Pilate to do so. Joseph wraps the body of Jesus in a new linen shroud and lays it in his freshly hewn tomb. Two Marys—Mary Magdalene and possibly Mary the mother of James (see Luke 24:10)—keep vigil that evening over the tomb until darkness falls, the Sabbath begins, and they return home (27:61; 28:1).

Meanwhile the Jewish authorities, having accomplished their desired end of removing Jesus, are frightened that he might reappear, for they have heard his prediction that he would rise again. They therefore ask for a guard to be set on the tomb, in case—as they say—the disciples steal the body and make out Jesus is alive (27:62–66). Their small-mindedness will, as we know, be overwhelmed by something far more wonderful—a permanent reversal of the old order, not a tacky pretence that deceitful disciples have overcome it.

The resurrection of Jesus

The world holds its breath for two days until the day after the Sabbath, a day that itself records the end of the old creation (see Genesis 2:2–3). The point is that the occurrence of the resurrection on the first day of the week begins a re-creation of humanity and the universe. Once again, accompanying signs attend this day of universal significance. There is a violent earthquake (28:2). An angel rolls the stone away, sits on it and overwhelms the guard. His clothes are "white as snow" (28:2–4). He addresses the women who are the first witnesses and the first evangelists of the empty tomb (28:5–7). They are to go and tell the disciples that Jesus has risen from the dead and will meet them in Galilee (although there are preliminary meetings in Jerusalem and on the road to Emmaus with other disciples). Jesus then meets the departing women, presumably having already encountered Mary Magdalene in the garden (see John 20:10–18). They worship him, holding on to his feet (28:9). Jesus gives them the same message as the angel: to tell the disciples that they will see him in Galilee, although he will in fact meet them that night in Jerusalem.

He calls the disciples his "brothers" (28:10) for the first time. They are part of, or will be part of, a new resurrection community.

Matthew's account of the resurrection is sparse—not quite as sparse as Mark's, but then it seems that the true ending of Mark's Gospel has been lost, and a new and different one attached.[102] Matthew's account is brief compared with Luke's and John's, but it is radical and single-minded. It is radical because the initial witnesses of the resurrection in Matthew are women, thereby elevating the significance of women in this new community. It is single-minded because the main message is that Jesus will meet with his disciples in Galilee as their resurrected Lord. The angel by the tomb first says this, then Jesus says the same. The stage is almost set for the final culmination of the Gospel. Before that happens, there is one more shoddy piece of human work to be done (28:11–15).

The earthquake-struck guards make their way into the city to give an account to their employers, the chief priests, of what has happened. News of the earthquake, the disappearance of the body of Jesus and the appearance of an angel so rattle the authorities that, having spent thirty pieces of silver for Jesus' arrest, they now spend a far greater sum to alter the evidence. The guards are to say that the disciples have taken the body and are just pretending Jesus is alive. It became, Matthew says, a persistent rumour, but it does not account for the extraordinary change in the disciples or their inspired and passionate preaching of the resurrection. Bribes cannot falsify the truth, nor the reality and hope of the resurrection. It is a flimsy deceit.

Matthew's Gospel concludes back in Galilee (28:16–20), where the ministry of Jesus began, if not his birth. They meet now on a mountain or hill, where great biblical moments of theophany and revelation have so often taken place. Most of the disciples worship him, but some doubt, for they are uncertain who this familiar-yet-unfamiliar, post-resurrection Jesus is, and are unsure of the significance of his resurrection. Nevertheless, it is now that Jesus declares, "All authority in heaven and on earth has been given to me" (28:18). In these words we come to the fulfilment of Jesus' kingship. It is not a local Judean kingship, but a universal one. It is not partial, but total; nothing is left outside the remit of his power. This statement fulfils Matthew's presentation of Jesus throughout the Gospel as the one who has all authority, and is the fulfilment of all that has been promised. In light of this authority, which is to be an ever-increasing reality on the earth, the disciples are to go throughout the world and among all nations, making disciples, baptizing in the threefold name of the Trinity—Father, Son and Spirit—and teaching new disciples to observe all that Jesus has taught. Disciples are to be *made*, *marked* by baptism, and then *matured* as believers. This great mission is to be accomplished in light of two things: his authority and his presence, for "surely I will be with you always, to the very end of the age." Just ten days later this process begins with explosive force at Pentecost, when three thousand people from many different regions are baptized in the name of the Father, the Son and the Holy Spirit in a single day (Acts 2:38–41). The fulfilment of God's great plan of salvation, promised in the Hebrew scriptures and centred on the coming of Jesus and his kingdom, is irresistibly taking place.

Group Discussion Questions

Chapter 1: Discovering the True Identity of Jesus

Matthew 1–4:11

1. How does Matthew go about identifying Jesus in this "book of origin"?
2. Why does he begin with a genealogy? What aspect of this genealogy appeals to you?
3. What is admirable about Joseph's conduct towards Mary?
4. Why is Matthew's nativity account so different from Luke's? What do you think was Matthew's main aim in telling it the way he did?
5. What does the journey of the Magi add to Matthew's account? Why did he include this story?
6. What do you especially like about the Magi's visit? What does their visit add to the nativity?
7. Why is the escape to Egypt an important piece of typology (Old Testament resonance) in Matthew's account? How would it resonate with a Jewish Christian?
8. What significance does Herod's opposition add to the nativity story?
9. What would we lack if we did not have Matthew's nativity account?
10. What else does John the Baptist's teaching add to our understanding of the identity of Jesus (3:1–17)?

Chapter 2: Laying the Foundations

Matthew 3:18–4:25

1. In what ways are foundations important to ministry? What kind of foundations do we look for, and why?
2. Why did Jesus get baptized? In what ways is Jesus' baptism different from or the same as our own baptism? What does your baptism mean to you?
3. What was the point of the temptations Jesus endured? How did they take place? What was unique to Jesus in these temptations? How did he combat them?
4. Why did Jesus fast? What place does fasting have in our spiritual discipline?
5. What was at the heart of Jesus' preaching?
6. Why did Jesus call these first disciples? What was his strategy in this? Why didn't he minister all alone, without the bother of disciples who wouldn't understand? How is fellowship important to you?
7. What lay at the heart of Jesus' ministry? What was the effect?

Chapter 3: Fulfilling the Calling of Discipleship

Matthew 5:1–16; 6:1–7:34

1. What is your favourite Beatitude, and why?
2. Which Beatitude is the most difficult to "*be*", and why?
3. What do you think is the purpose of the Beatitudes?
4. Why did Jesus choose the metaphors of salt and light to describe Christians?
5. What pitfalls are we to guard against in the spiritual disciplines of giving, praying and fasting?
6. When is it good to fast? How does it help?
7. What attitudes should we have towards wealth?
8. Why do we live in such an anxious society?

9. Is there such a thing as just criticism? Why should we be wary of judging people? Why is it easier to see other people's faults than our own?
10. What is the secret of fruitfulness?
11. Which spiritual discipline do you want to grow in presently?

Chapter 4: Jesus and the Fulfilment of the Law

Matthew 5:17–48

1. In what ways is Jesus' teaching here a fulfilment of the Old Testament law? What do you think Jesus meant by coming "to fulfil the law"?
2. Why do you think Jesus chose to extend the application of the laws against murder, adultery and divorce? What would be the effect of this extension?
3. Why do you think we have become a more angry society (road rage, air rage, Internet rage, and so on)?
4. When is the boundary crossed between admiration and lust in sexual desire? Is there a legitimate place for sexual desire?
5. Is there ever a place for reinforcing our speech with oaths?
6. Is Jesus' teaching on doing good to those who harm or exploit us realistic?
7. Is it good always to give to those who want to beg or borrow from you? What guides your response?
8. How do you love your enemies?

Chapter 5: The Presence of the Future

Matthew 8 and 9

1. What place should healing have in the Church today?
2. What do we learn about the healing ministry of Jesus in these two chapters?

3. What is the relationship between healing and the kingdom of God?

4. What is the difference between deliverance and healing?

5. Why do you think Matthew is so terse in his telling of some of these healing stories, compared with Mark and Luke?

6. When does faith come into play in these healing miracles, and when does it not? Why the difference?

7. What did Jesus fulfil from the Old Testament in relation to healing?

8. Teaching, preaching and healing seem to summarize Jesus' ministry. Is that the same for the Church today, and if so, how would you expect it to be worked out in a local Christian community?

9. Why are labourers always needed for the harvest field?

10. What particular insight would you want to emphasize from these two chapters (Matthew 8 and 9)?

Chapter 6: The Authority of Jesus

Matthew 8:23–27; 11:25–30; 12:15–21; 14:22–36; 14:13–21; 15:29–39
(Read through these different passages in your group to
build up a picture of Jesus' Galilean ministry.)

1. How is the authority of Jesus displayed in these early chapters of Matthew?

2. If there had been no lake in Galilee, what would Jesus' ministry have lacked (8:23–27; 14:22–33)?

3. What lessons for discipleship were learnt by the disciples as they travelled around in boats?

4. What are the principal lessons from the feeding of the four and the five thousand (14:13–21; 15:32–39)?

5. What is your idea of perfect rest? How does Christ give rest to our souls? What is the yoke that is easy like (11:28–30)?

6. What is your idea of the perfect Sabbath? How do we ensure rest in our modern way of life? How can we give life to others? (12:1–14)

7. What would the Church look like if it had the authority of Jesus today?
8. What is the difference between gentleness and weakness? And what does humility look like (11:25–30)?
9. What do bruised reeds and smouldering wicks need (12:15–21)?
10. Why is calling the Holy Spirit evil and calling evil good an unforgivable blasphemy (12:22–37)?
11. What is unique about Jesus' authority?

Chapter 7: Parables of the Kingdom

Matthew 13:1–58

1. Why did Jesus teach the crowds in parables? How does a parable work?
2. What are the main lessons from the Parable of the Sower? What is the difference between the different types of soil? How do these lessons from the Parable of the Sower help us?
3. Why did Jesus tell the Parables of the Wheat and Tares, and of the Fishing Net?
4. How do the Parables of the Treasure Hidden in the Field and the Pearl of Great Price differ? What truths do they convey?
5. How do we "bring out old and new" as good scribes? What does that amount to?
6. Why was Jesus rejected in his hometown?

Chapter 8: Jesus and John the Baptist

Matthew 3:1–17; 11:1–19; 14:1–23

1. Why is John the Baptist such an important figure in the Gospels?
2. What was the wisdom in having a forerunner to Jesus?
3. What was the effect of imprisonment on John the Baptist?
4. What are the causes of doubt? Is that something we experience?

5. How did Jesus deal with John's uncertainty?
6. What were the special characteristics of John's ministry?
7. Why is the least in the kingdom greater than John? Greater in what sense?
8. What effect might the execution of John have had on Jesus?
9. Why is solitary prayer so important at times (see 14:13,23)?

Chapter 9: The Watershed of the Gospel

Matthew 16:13–28

1. Why did Jesus want formal recognition of his identity?
2. What was so significant about this "confession" at Caesarea Philippi?
3. In what way was it different from previous confessions of Jesus as Messiah or Son of God?
4. How could Peter have got it so right and then so wrong?
5. Why was a crucified Messiah such a stumbling block to the Jews and folly to the Gentiles (1 Corinthians 1:23)?
6. In what way was this event a watershed in the Gospel?
7. How can people today recognize that Jesus is God's Son? What are the main barriers to this happening? What, humanly, enabled you to believe?
8. What overall lessons does this passage teach us?

Chapter 10: God's New Community

It would be wise either to divide this section up into two studies
(e.g. Matthew 10 and 17 could be one study, and Matthew 18 and
19:1–20:35 the other), or to get the group to read all five chapters
before a study on all this material—although that could be unwieldy!

Part I

1. What are the most striking instructions that Jesus gives the apostles when sending them out on their missionary expedition (10:1–42)?
2. What are the disciples to do and to avoid, and what can we learn from that for our own day (10:5–15)?
3. Why has the Church been so beset with persecution? What is the cause of such persecution when Christians are peace-loving, law-abiding citizens (10:16–24)?
4. Why is persecution or antipathy from your own household the most difficult (10:34–39)?
5. What comfort can God give to those facing such trials (10:26–33 and 10:40–42)?
6. What lessons are there for the Church in Matthew 17 from the transfiguration? From the failure to restore the boy? From the temple tax?

Part II

1. Who is the greatest in the kingdom of heaven, and why?
2. How do we treat temptations to sin (18:7–9)?
3. How is the compassion of God shown in the Parable of the Lost Sheep (18:10–14)? What does Matthew's use of this parable in the context of pastoral care tell us about Matthew as an editor?
4. How can we help to restore those who have wandered away from their faith?
5. What is the wisdom of Jesus' method of solving disputes (18:15–20)?

6. Why can forgiveness be so difficult (18:21–35)?

7. It was not so long ago that Edward VIII abdicated because he wanted to marry a divorced woman, and the Queen's sister, Princess Margaret, was forced to give up Peter Townsend, because he would have to divorce to marry her. When do you think people should be permitted to divorce (19:1–12)?

8. What was the attitude of Jesus to little children, and why (19:13–15)?

9. Why did Matthew place the story of the rich young ruler here in a discourse about church life (19:16–30), and likewise the Parable of the Labourers in the Vineyard (20:1–16)?

10. The discourse ends with Jesus again prophesying his impending death. Two episodes follow this prophecy before Jesus rides into Jerusalem to die. In what ways are the request from the mother of James and John and the healing of the blind beggars fitting precursors to what will follow (20:20–34)?

Chapter 11: Mercy, not Sacrifice

Matthew 9:9–17; 12:1–14; 15:1–20; 16:5–12; 23:1–39

1. What are the strengths and weaknesses of the spirituality of the Pharisees as presented in the Gospel of Matthew?

2. From the passages being studied in this section, what were the main points at issue between Jesus and the Pharisees and teachers of the law?

3. What were the grounds for Jesus describing the Pharisees and teachers of the law as hypocrites? What are hypocrites? Aren't all sinful human beings likely to be hypocrites? What is the likelihood of Christians being routinely accused of hypocrisy? Who is in danger of being called a hypocrite in churches?

4. When Jesus said that the Pharisees were to think about God wanting "mercy", and not "sacrifice", what did he (and the earlier prophets) mean? In what ways might we be in danger of putting sacrifice before mercy?

5. What basic diagnosis of the human condition did the Pharisees and others overlook (15:18–19)? Why did they do it? Why is Christianity different in this respect from most human philosophies (such as Marxism), which say that if we change the conditions or environment then we change people?

6. How would you describe the yeast of the Pharisees (16:5–12)? How can such a yeast spread in a church community?

7. What would you say are the main differences between the spirituality proposed by Jesus and the one condemned by Jesus in the "woes" (23:13–32)?

8. What were the main reasons Jesus could not gather together the people of Jerusalem, "as a mother hen gathers her chicks" (23:37)?

9. If you were to summarize in one phrase the difference between Jesus and the Pharisees or teachers of the law, what would it be? And how can we guard ourselves against becoming like the Pharisees?

Chapter 12: Fulfilling the Future

Matthew 24 and 25

1. What are the dangers to faith in fine religious buildings, and what are their good effects (24:1–2)?

2. What were the years leading up to the destruction of the temple going to be like? How were Jesus' followers to prepare for them?

3. How important is it to remember the return of Jesus (the *parousia*)? What kind of difference should it make to our living?

4. Why is there such a fascination with calculating when the Second Coming or *parousia* will be (24:36)?

5. What will be the characteristics of Jesus' return? What will be the signs that precede it?

6. What qualities is Jesus looking for in his disciples as they await his return? What are the main lessons from the five parables that Jesus tells? (*It may be helpful to divide into five groups or pairs and study a parable each, then report back the findings.*)

7. *How* are the main lessons taught by these parables? Those of the Talents, and of the Sheep and the Goats are probably the most compelling. How might they relate to each other? And how might the Parable of the Bridesmaids and the Oil Lamps relate to your conclusions about the above comparison?

8. In what way is our discipleship, or the practice of our faith, diminished by not having a clear understanding of the return of Christ?

Chapter 13: The Fulfilment of God's Plan

Once again in this chapter we are covering a lot of Scripture—and profound events, at that. It may be sensible to divide the material into two parts—Part I: Matthew 21 and 22; and Part II: Matthew 26, 27 and 28. Questions follow for each section or part.

Part 1: Matthew 21 and 22

1. What does the entry of Jesus into Jerusalem and his clearance of the temple tell us about his kingship, priorities and convictions? And what does that teach us about how to lead and to pray?

2. What was Jesus' attitude to the temple? Can you explain how you reached that conclusion?

3. When is it right to be angry? When is it wrong to be angry?

4. What do we learn from the parables that Jesus told here (the enacted Parable of the Fig Tree and the Parables of the Two Sons, of the Tenants, and of the Wedding Banquet)? Are they grouped together here for any particular reason?

5. How did these parables apply in Jesus' own day, and how do they apply now?

6. Why did Jesus face up to so many questions during these last few days of his ministry? Which of the five questions do you find most intriguing, and why? What do we learn about taxation, citizenship, marriage, and our main calling?

7. What kind of questions do we face as Christians, and how do we answer them?

Part II: Matthew 26–28

1. What was the purpose behind the anointing of Jesus in Bethany?
2. How does Judas find himself in the position of wanting to betray Jesus? What was the slippery slope that led him there?
3. What is the purpose of the Lord's Supper? How do we approach it, and what blessing do we receive from it?
4. How did Jesus use the time in Gethsemane, and how did the disciples *not* use it, especially Peter? What was Jesus struggling with there?
5. What are the chief lessons from the arrest of Jesus?
6. How did Jesus conduct himself during his two trials, before the High Priest/the Sanhedrin and before Pilate? What was the difference between the High Priest and Pilate? What in the end controlled them both?
7. What is the difference between the motivations and behaviour of Peter and Judas?
8. What does Matthew convey to us in his narrative of the crucifixion? What do we learn from his account about the death of Jesus and his inner suffering? What was happening when Jesus felt himself separated from the Father?
9. What were the various responses to Jesus' crucifixion? Do they correspond to any responses today?
10. How does the temple feature in what Matthew writes about the crucifixion?
11. Why were the women braver than the men (compare 26:56b and 27:55–56)?
12. What is the significance of the burial of Jesus?
13. What are the main features of Matthew's account of the resurrection?
14. How did the authorities seek to frustrate the resurrection?
15. What lies at the heart of the Great Commission (28:16–20)? How are we involved in fulfilling it?
16. And finally, what has been the abiding message for you from Matthew's Gospel?

Notes

1   Patrick Whitworth, *Gospel for the Outsider: The Gospel in Luke & Acts* (Durham: Sacristy Press, 2014).

2   The reader can consult the three-volume commentary of 1,500 pages by W. D. Davies and Dale C. Allison, Jr, published by T&T Clark in the International Critical Commentary series (1988–1997), or R. T. France's long and excellent commentary, *The Gospel of Matthew*, in the New International Commentary on the New Testament (NICNT) series (Grand Rapids, MI: Eerdmans, 2007).

3   R. T. France, *Matthew: An Introduction and Commentary*, Tyndale New Testament Commentaries series (Downers Grove, IL and Nottingham: IVP, 2008; first published 1985), p. 18.

4   France, *Matthew* (Tyndale), pp. 21–22.

5   James D. G. Dunn, *Neither Jew nor Greek: A Contested Identity*, Volume 3 of *Christianity in the Making* (Grand Rapids, MI and Cambridge, UK: Eerdmans, 2015), pp. 246–247.

6   Dunn, *Neither Jew nor Greek*, pp. 199,247.

7   Dunn, *Neither Jew nor Greek*, p. 201.

8   Eusebius, *Historia Ecclesiastica* III.39.15, tr. G. A. Williamson (London: Penguin Books, 1989), p. 104.

9   France, *Matthew* (Tyndale), p. 33.

10 Origen was the greatest biblical commentator of the third century, who in the second half of his career lived and ministered in Caesarea and wrote the first known commentary on Matthew. He accepted Matthew's authorship.

11 France, *Matthew* (Tyndale), p. 31.

12 Jack Dean Kingsbury, *Matthew: Structure, Christology, Kingdom* (Philadelphia: Fortress Press, 1975).

13 B. W. Bacon, "The Five Books of Matthew Against the Jews", *The Expositor* 15 (1918), pp. 56–66.

[14] "New creation" is the term preferred by W. D. Davies and Dale C. Allison Jr in *A Critical and Exegetical Commentary on the Gospel According to Saint Matthew*, Vol. 1 (Edinburgh: T&T Clark, 1988), p. 150.

[15] France, *Matthew* (NICNT), p. 29.

[16] Ibid.

[17] France, *Matthew* (NICNT), p. 37.

[18] Eduard Schweizer, *The Good News According to Matthew*, tr. David E. Green (Atlanta: John Knox Press, 1975), p. 25.

[19] Joseph Ratzinger, Pope Benedict XVI, *Jesus of Nazareth: The Infancy Narratives*, tr. Philip J. Whitmore (London: Bloomsbury, 2012), p. 39.

[20] Greek "*enthymethentos*": see Ratzinger, *Infancy Narratives*, p. 41.

[21] Edward R. Hardy (ed.), *Christology of the Later Fathers* (5th edition, London: Westminster Press, 1954), p. 364.

[22] France, *Matthew* (NICNT), p. 69.

[23] Nazarene is not the same as Nazirite, which alludes to a vow of abstinence (taken, for example, by Samson in the Old Testament: see Judges 13:5,7;16:17).

[24] France, *Matthew* (NICNT), p. 95.

[25] France, *Matthew* (NICNT), p. 120.

[26] Gregory of Nyssa, *On the Difference between Essence and Hypostasis*, quoted in Kallistos Ware, *The Orthodox Way* (New York: St Vladimir's Seminary Press, 1995), p. 31.

[27] Craig S. Keener, *A Commentary on the Gospel of Matthew* (Grand Rapids, MI and Cambridge, UK: Eerdmans, 1999), p. 141.

[28] The Septuagint was reputedly compiled in Alexandria by seventy Jewish scholars in the third century BC.

[29] Zebulun is a son of Leah, the sister of Jacob's beloved Rachel, while Naphtali is a son of Bilhah, Rachel's maid; see Genesis 46:14,24.

[30] See France, *Matthew* (NICNT), p.151.

[31] France, *Matthew* (Tyndale), p.111.

[32] France, *Matthew* (NICNT), p. 159.

[33] France, *Matthew* (Tyndale), p. 114.

[34] France, *Matthew* (NICNT), p. 166.

[35] Augustine, *Sermons*, 61.4.

[36] W. D. Davies, *The Gospel and the Land: Early Christianity and Jewish Territorial Doctrine* (Berkeley, CA: University of California Press, 1974), p. 362, cited in France, *Matthew* (NICNT), p. 167, footnote 25.

37 William Shakespeare, *The Merchant of Venice*, Act IV, Scene I.

38 Origen, *On Prayer*, tr. William A. Curtis (London: Aeterna Press, 2015), chapter xvii, "Give us today our needful bread".

39 See, for example, the monastic life in the fourth century of Jerome and Eustochium in Bethlehem; Patrick Whitworth, *From Constantinople to Chalcedon: The Shaping of the World to Come* (Durham: Sacristy Press, 2017), pp. 278ff.

40 See Paula Gooder, *Body: Biblical Spirituality for the Whole Person* (London: SPCK, 2016).

41 Dunn, *Neither Jew nor Greek*, pp. 686–694.

42 France, *Matthew* (NICNT), p. 183.

43 "*Raca*" is an Aramaic term of contempt, meaning something like "empty-headed". See France, *Matthew* (NICNT), p. 201, footnote 83.

44 France, *Matthew* (NICNT), p. 204.

45 See Augustine, Basil of Caesarea, and Jerome. Whitworth, *From Constantinople to Chalcedon*, p. 199.

46 France, *Matthew* (NICNT), p. 221.

47 See <https://www.torturedforchrist.com/about/who-was-richard-wurmbrand/> (accessed 7 April 2019).

48 The word used is "*proskunei*", one of the most common and intimate words for worship in the New Testament.

49 France, *Matthew* (NICNT), p. 339.

50 El Koursi is probably the present day location of Gadara, where there is now a ruin of a fifth-century church, known to Origen and Eusebius of Caesarea in the third and fourth centuries respectively.

51 France, *Matthew* (NICNT), pp. 456–457. *[Please check these page numbers.]*

52 France, *Matthew* (NICNT), p. 455.

53 France, *Matthew* (NICNT), p. 464; France, *Matthew* (Tyndale), p. 208. For more about the Qumran community, see pp. 96.

54 Joachim Jeremias, *The Parables of Jesus* (3rd edition, London: SCM, 1972), p. 150.

55 France, *Matthew* (NICNT), pp. 525–526.

56 Jeremias, *Parables of Jesus*, p. 149.

57 France, *Matthew* (NICNT), p. 543.

58 Josephus, *Antiquities* 18.116–119.

59 France, *Matthew* (NICNT), p. 98.

[60]   Ibid.

[61]   See Whitworth, *From Constantinople to Chalcedon*, p. 295.

[62]   Dietrich Bonhoeffer, *Letters and Papers from Prison*, ed. Eberhard Bethge (London: Collins Fontana, 1970), pp. 28–29 (my italics).

[63]   Os Guinness, *Doubt* (London: Lion Publishing, 1976), pp. 117–131.

[64]   Guinness, *Doubt*, p. 118.

[65]   Isaiah 4:2–6 refers to the "Branch of the Lord", who will be "beautiful and glorious" and will unite the survivors of Israel; in Isaiah 11 the Messiah (not so named) is described as the "Branch from Jesse" or "Root of Jesse" on whom will rest the Spirit of the Lord: "the Spirit of wisdom and of understanding, the Spirit of counsel and of power, the Spirit of knowledge and of the fear of the Lord—and he will delight in the fear of the Lord" (Isaiah 11:2–3).

[66]   See 4Q174 *Florilegium* and 4Q246 *Aramaic Apocalypse*: both are part of the Dead Sea Scrolls, Qumran literature—France, *Matthew* (NICNT), p. xxiv.

[67]   France, *Matthew* (NICNT), p. 619.

[68]   France, *Matthew* (NICNT), p. 627.

[69]   Jim Elliot's diary entry, 28 October 1949.

[70]   Whitworth, *Gospel for the Outsider*.

[71]   France, *Matthew* (NICNT), p. 384.

[72]   For further discussion see France, *Matthew* (NICNT), p.384.

[73]   See Russ Parker, *Rediscovering the Ministry of Blessing* (London: SPCK, 2014) and Graham Tomlin, *The Widening Circle* (London: SPCK, 2014).

[74]   See Augustine, *Sermons*, 61.4.

[75]   See France, *Matthew* (NICNT), p. 685.

[76]   The dispute between the Rabbinic schools concerns what this "indecency" might amount to.

[77]   France, *Matthew* (NICNT), p. 714.

[78]   France, *Matthew* (NICNT), p. 723.

[79]   France, *Matthew* (Tyndale), p. 172.

[80]   See France, *Matthew* (NICNT), p. 354.

[81]   See also Jeremiah 7:4–11; Amos 5:21–24; Micah 6:6–8; 1 Samuel 15:22; Psalms 50:7–15; 51:16–17.

[82]   "*Qorban*" is a way of devoting food, money or property to God—in effect, to the temple treasury—through a vow, thereby putting it beyond the reach of parents or relatives. Thus parents cannot benefit from these resources if *Qorban* is invoked.

[83] See also Matthew's record of judgement on unrepentant towns in 11:20–24; or on those who cause others to stumble in 18:7b; or on Judas in 26:24.

[84] Josephus, *The Jewish War*, tr. G. A. Williamson (London: Penguin, 1972), pp. 232ff.

[85] Josephus, *Jewish War* (London: Penguin, 1969), pp. 276–277.

[86] France, *Matthew* (NICNT), p. 902.

[87] In a previous era, Antiochus Epiphanes and Pompey, in 168 BC and 63 BC respectively, both desecrated the temple by bringing their pagan regalia into its courts. The sacrilege of Antiochus Epiphanes is referred to in Daniel 9:27; 11:31; 12:11.

[88] See France, *Matthew* (NICNT), p. 919.

[89] C. S. Lewis, *Mere Christianity* (London: Fount Collins 1981), p. 62.

[90] See the conversation between Jesus and Peter about "feed[ing] my sheep" in John 21:15–19.

[91] Kenneth E. Bailey, *Jesus through Middle Eastern Eyes* (London: SPCK, 2008), p. 273.

[92] See Bailey, *Jesus through Middle Eastern Eyes*, p. 398.

[93] France, *Matthew* (Tyndale), p. 303.

[94] France, *Matthew* (NICNT), p. 782.

[95] The verses from Isaiah emphasize that all nations, foreigners and exiles come to the temple for prayer.

[96] Levirate duty demands that a brother should marry his brother's widow to give offspring to his name, and that the widow should marry one of her husband's brothers.

[97] Note that in verse 32 Jesus returns to the image of the fig tree.

[98] For a more detailed explanation of this, read Romans 9—11.

[99] For a full discussion of the dating of the Passover meal, see France, *Matthew* (NICNT), pp. 981–983, or France, *Matthew* (Tyndale), pp. 369–370).

[100] J. R. W. Stott, *The Cross of Christ* (Leicester: InterVarsity Press, 1986), p. 156.

[101] Athanasius, *De Incarnatione*, Section 54, ed. Robert W. Thomson, Oxford Early Christian Texts (Oxford: Clarendon Press, 1971), p. 269.

[102] France, *Matthew* (NICNT), p. 1097, footnote 17.